Advance Praise for *When*

"Dr. Ken Adams has done it again. This book on mother-son enmeshment explains not only this too little understood developmental block, but points the way to liberation. The absence of psychobabble makes it clear reading both for victims and their clinicians."

— John Franklin, Ph.D., Distinguished Professor of Counseling and Addiction Studies, University of Detroit Mercy

"An engaging, clear, and extremely useful examination of this most common of family problems....I do a lot of couples therapy in my practice, and this is one of the most common unhealthy dynamics I see. This book will be enormously helpful."

— John C. Friel, Ph.D., author of *Adult Children*

"It is a compelling, insightful, and helpful guide out of the sexual and romantic labyrinths families weave."

— Patrick J. Carnes, Ph.D., author of *Out of the Shadows*

ALSO BY KENNETH M. ADAMS, PH.D.

Silently Seduced

When He's Married to MOM

∽

How to Help Mother-Enmeshed Men Open Their Hearts to TRUE LOVE and COMMITMENT

KENNETH M. ADAMS, PH.D.,
with ALEXANDER P. MORGAN

A Fireside Book
Published by Simon & Schuster
New York London Toronto Sydney

FIRESIDE
Rockefeller Center
1230 Avenue of the Americas
New York, NY 10020

FIRESIDE and colophon are registered trademarks
of Simon & Schuster, Inc.

For information about special discounts for bulk purchases,
please contact Simon & Schuster Special Sales
at 1-800-456-6798 or business@simonandschuster.com.

Designed by Mary Austin Speaker

Manufactured in the United States of America

10   9   8   7   6   5   4   3   2   1

Library of Congress Cataloging-in-Publication Data
Adams, Kenneth M.
    When he's married to mom : how to help mother-enmeshed men open their hearts to true love and
commitment / Kenneth M. Adams, with Alexander P. Morgan.
      p.   cm.
    Includes index.
      1. Mothers and sons.   2. Men—Psychology.   3. Love—Psychological aspects.
    4. Commitment (Psychology)   I. Morgan, Alexander P.   II. Title.
HQ755.85.A33 2007
155.9'24—dc22   2006048844

ISBN-13: 978-0-7432-9138-5

DISCLAIMER

In my twenty-five years of practice, I have helped priests and politicians, media personalities and teachers, military men and medical doctors. Their case stories have informed and inspired the stories in this book. Of course, all real names and situations have been changed to maintain the anonymity of my clients. Often the stories are composites and combinations of real stories, for clarity as well as anonymity. If it appears that some-one discussed in this book is identifiable in the real world, please be assured that this is merely coincidental.

To Cheryl and Zachary, the love and joy of my life
KMA

To Janice, Abraham, and Julia, my reason for being
APM

ACKNOWLEDGMENTS

Many people have influenced the development of this book. I am particularly grateful to the men, and the women who have loved them, who found their way to my office and shared their heartfelt stories. Their struggles and paths of healing served as the basis for *When He's Married to Mom.*

Dr. Patrick Carnes's review and endorsement of an early draft of the book helped reassure me I was on the right track. His mentoring and friendship over the years have been a great support to me. He has helped show me how to handle difficult topics many would rather not talk about. Dr. John Friel also reviewed an early draft and offered an enthusiastic endorsement. He, too, has been a valuable mentor and friend. He was particularly encouraging when I first began studying and writing about enmeshment many years ago. I am deeply grateful to them both.

Dr. Mark Schwartz has contributed an enormous body of research and clinical observations on the relationship between early attachment failure and later intimacy and sexual problems. His work has served as an important barometer for me over the course of my writing and clinical practice. It was critical to my thinking in laying the theoretical foundation for the book.

Dr. Joe and Shirley Bavonese and Carol Ross reviewed an early draft of the book and gave helpful feedback. Janice Morgan provided the working title *Married to Mom* for the book. Dr. Martha Turner and Judith Matheny have reminded me regularly about the importance of my writing and work in this area. Dr. Alyson Nerenberg, Bob Dilbeck, Richard Sorensen, Paul and Ginny Hartman, Charley Schults, and Eric Griffin-Shelly have also encouraged me. My good friend Carl Schuman reviewed and offered important feedback on an early draft and has generously offered his support of my work over the years. I am thankful to them all.

My associates Don Robinson, Connie Stephenson, Dr. Judith Trenkamp, and Judy Norwood offered invaluable support, wisdom, and insight regarding the enmeshment cases we treated. I am grateful to be working with such a competent group of colleagues.

My wife, Cheryl, provided encouragement and accommodation for the time I needed for this project in a schedule that was already too tight for more. She also reviewed and offered helpful feedback of the book throughout. I am endlessly and lovingly grateful.

Alexander would like to thank Susan Schwartz, Penelope Franklin, and Irene Prokop for valuable suggestions to improve the proposal for this book, while it was in early stages of development. He also appreciates the opportunity to "pitch" the book at the Mid-Atlantic Creative Nonfiction Summer Writers' Conference in 2004. He would like to thank the conference director, Lee Gutkind, and his workshop leader, Dinty Moore, for their encouragement. He wants especially to acknowledge the hard work and beyond-duty dedication of Susan Schwartz for reviewing parts of the first draft. It is a much better book for her efforts. Finally, he sends love and appreciation to his wife, Janice, for all her encouragement and support.

We both would like to thank our agent, Jane Dystel, for her recognition of the importance of the book and her expert guidance throughout. We are also thankful to Miriam Goderich for her guidance and encouragement. We are very grateful to our editor at Fireside, Cherise Davis, for her enthusiasm and insights. Together, they championed and guided the project. We appreciate all of their efforts.

CONTENTS

A LOSS OF FREEDOM:
THE ENMESHMENT TRAP

Over the course of my twenty-five years of clinical practice, I have worked with and successfully treated hundreds of men who have excessive emotional ties to their mothers. They feel trapped, guilty, and disloyal when attempting to follow their own wishes and lead their own lives. I refer to this syndrome as mother-son enmeshment; those who suffer from it are mother-enmeshed men, MEM for short. (I also use MEM for the singular "mother-enmeshed man.") Often these men are portrayed in books, movies, and television as weak and indecisive. There is little awareness that they have been damaged and that enmeshment is a major cause.

MEM are commitment phobic. Women who love them are often frustrated that their lovers will travel only so far down the road of courtship before they get stuck. At the beginning of the relationship, these men are so exciting, so loving, so considerate . . . then the connection suddenly loses all its energy. The men back away and won't explain why. They won't commit!

From the man's perspective, however, it is not that he *won't* commit but that he *can't* commit. His childhood relationship with his mother—embedded now in his unconscious as a template controlling his behavior—won't allow him to get serious about someone else.

Most close relationships between mothers and sons are not

enmeshed relationships. The key distinction is that, in a healthy mother-son connection, the son's needs are being addressed and the mother meets her own needs for emotional support and companionship elsewhere. In an enmeshed relationship, the mother uses her son for emotional support and companionship. He learns to focus on keeping her satisfied. He becomes her surrogate husband. Struggling under this burden, he is drained of his youthful energy.

This book isn't about blaming mothers or trying to provoke guilt. It's about inviting mothers to free themselves and create emotional safety for their children, who will be able to grow up to have fulfilling lives and their own happy children.

Commitment phobia is one of the symptoms exhibited by MEM, but there are others. Many MEM feel *guilty* and *inadequate* and are bothered by *low self-worth*. They can also be *indecisive*. MEM are sometimes *people pleasers,* who help others at a severe cost to themselves. *Self-neglect* is another common symptom of MEM. Finally, when a MEM initiates therapy with me, it will often be to deal with the *addictions* and *sexual problems* that are common consequences of mother-son enmeshment.

It is estimated that one in ten men in this country have excessive ties to their mothers. This conservative estimate comes from established data on men sexually abused as children, male sex addicts, and adult children of alcoholics, where estimates of MEM can be made. For example, clinicians in national inpatient addiction treatment programs have estimated in informal surveys that up to 40 percent of male sex addicts have enmeshment issues with their mothers. Further, this enmeshment is seen as a significant factor in their sexually addictive behavior.

A clear profile has emerged for mother-enmeshed men. I explain the profile in Part One of this book and present case histories of seven different MEM in the first seven chapters. Each of these MEM manifests a different aspect of the MEM profile. Although these men and their partners and their stories are different, each is rooted in the dynamic of mother-son enmeshment. I would like the hopeful outcomes of these stories to encourage you by showing that your relationship is not as uniquely frustrating as it seems and that other couples have overcome similar problems. Chapter 8 summarizes the key points of Part One.

In Part Two we turn to you, the reader, and offer two chapters focusing on self-understanding, beginning with a questionnaire: "Are You a Mother-Enmeshed Man?" If you can't wait to evaluate yourself, you will find it at the beginning of Chapter 9.

Chapter 9 goes on to consider the astonishing influence that the unconscious mind has on our daily lives. Although the unconscious helps us decide whom we date, whom we make love to, and whom we marry, it often operates outside our awareness and our will. Self-understanding requires learning to observe unconscious influences and to heal unconscious wounds.

The unconscious is not always an unhealthy influence. When a childhood has been emotionally healthy, the unconscious operates as a functional silent partner. It doesn't intrude, and it can be helpful, for example, by giving access to creative energy and intuition. A foundation of healthy early experiences powers our joy, our willingness to bond with others, our ability to feel passion, and our healthy sexuality.

But a childhood marred by emotional damage establishes an unconscious mind that is intrusive. It holds the remnants of a child's unresolved conflicts, fears, and angers. It responds to these old injuries by acting them out, often to the harm of the adult the child becomes. Fortunately, the unconscious can be negotiated with and encouraged to express its story with less damage and a more positive outcome. Therapists are the guides in these negotiations, and the therapeutic journey is the only route that leads to this accommodation. For a MEM to get better, he must understand how enmeshment is limiting his life, how his unconscious mind influences his life, and how psychotherapy can change his life.

Chapter 10 discusses therapy: Who needs it. How to choose a therapist. What should happen in therapy. I have had much success with MEM in therapy, a fact that I hope carries a message of hope for healing to everyone reading this book.

Part Three is about relationships: how things can be made better for MEM and the people who love them. Since many of my MEM clients first came to see me at the urging of their wives, fiancées, or girlfriends, I include in Part Three specific advice for women involved with MEM.

Chapter 11 focuses on how to make relationships with parents and siblings into positive sources of support or, if that's impossible, to limit the damage. There is advice in Chapter 12 on romance and commitment for MEM and in Chapter 13 for women involved with MEM. Chapter 14 has guidelines for parents who want to avoid enmeshing their own children.

The good news for MEM, and the women who love them, is that help is possible. A MEM can be treated using a variety of techniques, including support groups and psychotherapy. With treatment, he can be freed from the painful inner conflicts that drive his "ambivalent" behavior. I've helped many MEM for whom commitment eventually became a liberating adventure rather than a burden. For the women involved with MEM, this book is a guide to what is going on with their men and how best to help them.

There is a universe of difference between a mother who loves her son dearly and a mother who makes her son the primary focus of her passion and preoccupation in an attempt to compensate for her own emptiness. I invite readers to clarify this distinction as they read this book and discover a message of hope, love, and freedom.

PART ONE

❦

What Are You Dealing With?

1 ANNE'S DILEMMA
The Man Who Won't Commit

Sonny and Anne sat on the front porch of his mother's house, talking in whispers. Anne felt almost beyond tears. Sonny sat beside her, confused.

"You'll never find a better woman than me," Anne was saying. "Except your mother, of course," she added, her anger breaking through to sarcasm.

"This isn't about my mother," Sonny said. He tried to explain, for what felt like the hundredth time. "So my mother relies on me. What's wrong with that? I'm her only son. She can't manage on her own. She needs to know I'm *there* for her."

Anne stood up, barely containing herself. "That's *not* what it's about! Your mother never lets you alone. She interrupts us day and night; you never say no to her." Anne walked toward the steps, pulling on her coat. "Go ahead, go take care of her! I've just about had it."

Sonny started after Anne, but then he stopped. He didn't know what to do. He knew he loved her, but . . . "You're being silly," he said. "This isn't her fault."

Just then the front door opened, and Sonny's mother, Ruth, leaned halfway out, clutching a flowered robe around her.

"Sonny," she said, ignoring Anne, "I forgot to tell you . . . the men to fix the lights are coming tomorrow afternoon."

Sonny stood up and put his arm around his mother. "That's good, Mom," he said. "I'm glad you're getting those bathroom lights fixed. That flickering is driving me crazy."

"So, you'll come maybe for lunch . . . then, when they show up, you'll tell them what's wrong?"

"I've got to work tomorrow, Mom. The men will know what to do, just show them the lights."

"I hate to be alone with strange men here. It makes me so nervous."

"Okay, Mom. Call me when they come, and I'll talk to them."

Ruth's lip quivered; then she shrugged. "If that's the best you can do. . . ." She shook her head and went back inside.

Anne was halfway down the steps. She turned around. "I love you, Sonny, but I'm thirty-five. I can't wait forever."

Sonny was beginning to feel guilty and angry, and these feelings scared him. "If you let me get away," Anne was saying, "twenty years from now, you'll regret losing the love of your life. And twenty years from now, regret will be all you have. But now . . . now you can do something about it."

"Anne," Sonny began, "What do you want me to say?"

"Make a decision. Say yes, say no, but don't keep me waiting like this."

Sonny stood, speechless. Something in him wanted to say no, just to get it over with. But, somehow, the word "regret" had struck a chord. Why couldn't he decide? He'd always been this way, and he hated it. It was so hard making decisions.

Anne sensed Sonny's desperation. She saw how stuck he

was. She didn't want to leave him, but she just couldn't take this anymore. Something had to give. What could she do?

Anne's Had Enough

Anne first came to see me a few weeks after her confrontation with Sonny on his mother's porch. *He* was too stuck to look for help, but *Anne* wanted answers. And she wasn't afraid to see someone about it.

She radiated competence and control, and I wasn't surprised when she told me she had gone to Yale Law School. She wanted to talk to me about her fiancé, she said, sitting down in my big leather chair and crossing her legs without relaxing.

"It's not that I'm whining," she began, "but he won't let us set a date for the wedding. He says he loves me, but I just can't pin him down. He always puts me off."

"What does he say?"

"Well, he's always very busy. It didn't start out like this. When we first met, he called me every day. We had dinner every night. He was smart, funny, and crazy about me. I said to myself: This is the man! He wants children. I want children. Let's get on with it."

"So then . . ." I suggested.

"And, so, well, nothing. We've settled into a once-a-week thing. We have fun when we're together. He says he loves me. But if I press him about marriage, he just puts me off."

"Is that something he does a lot," I asked, "put you off?"

Anne looked at me, suddenly a little less self-confident. She nodded.

"How does that make you feel?"

Anne recrossed her legs and found a corner of my office to

make eye contact with. "I'll tell you, it really made me question myself as a woman." She stopped and sighed. "I tried to find out if I had offended him, done something to make him back off, but he denies it." She paused. "And then there's his mother," she added. "He's very close to his mother."

"Too close?" I asked, when she didn't go on.

"We hardly ever have time together that isn't interrupted. She calls him on his cell phone, and, if he doesn't pick up, she pages him on his pager, which is supposed to be for emergencies. Last week we were having dinner out, and she called. He let her whine for forty-five minutes. Can you believe it? Our date was ruined, just because one of her neighbors left his garbage cans out on the curb too long."

"You sound angry," I suggested.

"I'm furious," she admitted, and began to cry. "I mean, I'm the woman he loves. I should have a *place* in his life, not *leftovers*."

She pulled herself together with the help of a Kleenex and went on.

"So I confronted him," she continued. " 'You can't commit to me because you've never let go of Mom,' I told him. 'But now it's time to set limits with her.' He didn't like that!" She laughed, but her eyes were sad. "He said I didn't understand. Now I feel trapped. If I push, he gets angry. If I try to get too close or too loving, he backs away. It's just that he's so focused on taking care of her. 'She needs someone to talk to,' he tells me, then he lets her talk his ear off.

"But am I crazy, or what? *His mother* makes me feel like a betrayed wife. I don't want to get in the way of his relationship with his mother, but is this normal? *He* says I'm making too much of it. It's *my* problem."

"No, you're not overreacting," I said. "What you're experiencing *is* what a betrayed wife would experience: rejection, anger, hurt. And, since the 'other woman' is Sonny's mother, feeling that you can't win is natural."

"I don't want to waste my life trying to get Sonny to commit," she said. "I need a reality check. Is he stuck where he's at? *Should I move on?*"

I couldn't answer that, but I did want to leave her with some clarity about her situation.

"You're feeling frustrated and helpless, with nowhere to go," I said. "What I know as a clinician is that he is trapped. He, too, has nowhere to go. He's up against his *Disloyalty Bind* (described in the box below), and he can't figure any way out. His solution is to distance himself from you, because distancing himself from his mother produces too much guilt. Then he blames you for not being understanding enough.

FUNDAMENTALS OF MEM:
The Disloyalty Bind

In his unconscious—and sometimes conscious—mind, a mother-enmeshed man (MEM) is representing his mother's interests, while his own have become secondary. If he does something he thinks she wouldn't like, he feels disloyal to her. If he "gets serious" about a woman, suddenly, without understanding why, he is overwhelmed with feelings of fear, anxiety, and guilt. Ambivalence and withdrawal inevitably follow.

"It's a terrible bind," I went on. "Unless he's willing to come for counseling, you have only two options: *accommodate* or *break up.* By accommodate, I mean stay connected to him but accept that Mom will always come first. Accommodation will likely make you feel resentful, and you may have to give up your dream of having a family, at least one where you would have a primary role. Sadly, breaking up becomes the reasonable alternative, if he's not willing to take a look at what's going on."

I paused. "When I share with women who come to see me what their men are up against, and therefore what *they* are up against, they become either relieved or depressed. The main thing I can do is make you aware of the importance of taking care of yourself and help you understand your options."

Anne was quiet for a while, thinking, taking it all in. Finally she gave me a little smile. "Being depressed isn't my style," she said, "so I guess I'll be relieved. What should I do now?"

When a MEM Wants a Wife

When a man is excessively bonded with his mother, what happens when he is looking for a wife? There are several common patterns; Sonny's story is one of the most common. He meets Anne, and initially he idealizes her. He cherishes her. He sweeps her off her feet. In this initial stage of courting, he is projecting onto Anne the very solicitous way he had learned to deal with his mother when he was a little boy. Then he discovers (unconsciously; he doesn't realize what is happening) that this new woman is competition for his mother, and the woman's got to go. Anne was once the object of his adoration. Now she becomes an object for his rejection. Naturally, she is devastated and confused. If she fights back by asking for clarity and commitment, he feels he's being pressured to be disloyal to his mother. Like a planet caught between two suns, the pull of his mother keeps him from getting close to Anne, while the pull of Anne is constant. This is what is so crazy-making for Anne. She knows that Sonny loves her. She can't understand what is keeping him from coming into her orbit. See Figure 1.1.

I sometimes use the movie *Psycho* to dramatize the Disloyalty Bind. There is a particular sequence of scenes in this movie when Norman first meets Marion. He takes a liking to her, and his mother is already having a problem with it. (Of course, his mother exists only in Norman's mind, but he vocalizes her comments offstage, so that we and Marion can hear.) Marion asks him, "Why do you let her treat you like that?" and immediately his face changes. Now he sees Marion as a threat. The movie dramatizes the mechanism that drives the behavior of a MEM: first comes his innocent, enthusiastic (sexual) interest in the attractive woman, then the interest provokes his Disloyalty Bind

The Disloyalty Bind

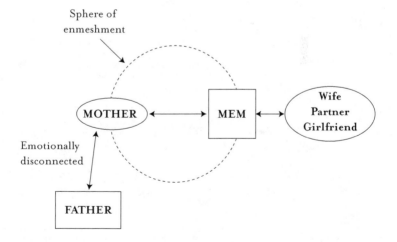

Figure 1-1. The constant pull on a MEM by his mother keeps him enmeshed and prevents him from following his natural desire to get close to his wife/partner/girlfriend. If his father and mother were emotionally connected, the enmeshment would be less likely to occur.

with this mother, and finally the object of the interest (the woman) has to be destroyed. The movie shows all this in a graphic and literal way.

Anne realizes that Sonny is too bound to his mother, because his mother is still active in his life. The fact that Sonny is not free to make time for Anne is clarified by his mother's actual interruptions. More mysterious and difficult to grasp is that sometimes the mother is nowhere to be seen but still has the same influence. Even if a man's mother is deceased, for example, the man's feelings of disloyalty to her might still be operating, preventing him from getting close to other women.

Here is the heart of the mystery: *The templates established by childhood relationships are an active overlay on adult relationships.* This fact is fundamental to understanding why a man who was enmeshed with his mother in childhood behaves the way he does. The fact that we are all haunted by shadows from the past can be difficult to comprehend. Generally, other people's ghosts are easier to see than our own.

In the specific case of a MEM, the remnants of the guilty bond to his mother can be so powerful that the man is frozen in the past, whether he talks to his mother every day or not for decades. He thinks he wants a loving wife, children, the optimism and labor of family life. But the anxiety he feels when he gets close to achieving this goal shuts him down. He cannot commit. He cannot leave. He is stuck. Or he moves on to the next woman, convinced it is his current girlfriend, and not his own ghosts, that is the problem.

He might imagine that he longs for "the perfect woman," but every time he finds her, she becomes "not perfect." He loses interest, and he wants somebody else he can imagine will be perfect. The pattern is often cyclical: seeking the perfect partner, idealizing the women he finds, dealing with disillusion-ment, struggling with commitment, seeking a new partner, and so on.

This repetitive pattern is a reflection and consequence of the story of his relationship with his mother. He idealized her and felt the exhilarating wonderment of being so special. He also felt guilty and angry and wanted distance from her. However, she would not permit him to express these feelings, and he learned to bury them. Instead, all these "forgotten" feelings—the guilt, the anger, the desire for distance—come up from his unconscious, when, as an adult, he gets too close to a woman.

The enmeshed relationship with his mother was not his choice. It was forced on him by the overwhelming circumstance of being a very little boy with a very needy mother. Despite the thrill and pleasure, he also knows at some level that she has smothered his autonomy. All of the anger and disappointment that he contained *then* is projected onto his partner *now,* and his attraction to her is tempered by an unconscious avoid-ance of getting too close. He becomes ambivalent. If nothing changes, he will never experience the full masculine pride of making his own choices, of having his own wife, of fathering his own children.

He Can't Hear Her

Sonny had a beard and an easy smile. There wasn't a trace of the resentment that I often see when a woman "drags" her man in for counseling. I let Anne set the scene, and she covered the same ground for Sonny she had covered with me.

"I love you, Sonny," she finished. "Are you really going to let your mother ruin our happiness?"

"You're not being fair," Sonny protested. "I have to take care of Mom." Turning to me, he said, "Anne is making too much of this."

"What I hear her saying," I replied, "is that she wants you to set aside some time for just the two of you. She wants a special place in your life."

"Right," he agreed, pulling at his beard, then looking to see if he had pulled out anything.

"Don't you love me?" Anne asked, with a suggestion of tremor behind the boldness.

"It isn't that easy," Sonny replied, shrinking back into his chair. "You can't just push me like that. I have to be ready."

The session continued, as I let Sonny and Anne repeat and clarify their points of view. Sonny was so focused on defending his mother's needs that what Anne was saying to him just didn't seem to penetrate. In some very real sense, he couldn't hear her. My clinical assessment was that the best next move would be some individual work with Sonny.

A week later Sonny came back without Anne.

"Tell me how you met Anne," I said, thinking this might be an easy way to get started.

Sonny brightened immediately. "She was so beautiful," he said, "and so self-confident. She just blew me away!"

Sonny had met Anne at a Fourth of July party given by mutual friends. Their attraction was immediate and powerful. They withdrew from the group to talk. They held hands. They laughed. The rest of the party faded into irrelevance.

When Sonny's pager went off at ten P.M., he almost allowed himself to ignore it. He took down Anne's number as he was leaving, sent roses to her law office the next day, and called her that evening.

The next two months were a thrilling romantic carnival ride, the surprise of found love by two people old enough to appreciate it. Now work, even long hours of work, was sanctified by the knowledge that they would be meeting in the evening.

The crash seemed to come out of nowhere. He began to notice that Anne was a little too opinionated. He decided he didn't like her brown suits or her burgundy nail polish. He wished she wouldn't look so disappointed when his mother called. And she wanted to get engaged. She was pretty pushy about it.

He felt a kind of panic. He didn't want to say no to getting engaged, because he didn't want to displease her, but he just wasn't sure he wanted to commit. Even so, he didn't want to break up. He was caught in ambivalence.

"Tell me about your mother," I said, glad for the opportunity to explore the topic.

"She depends on me," Sonny said. "She always has."

"Even when you were little?" I asked.

"Yes," he agreed. "Even then."

His Mother's Only Friend

The growing emotional distance between Sonny's parents was marked by divorce when he was eight years old. His parents were amiable and acted like it was no big deal, but when his father was gone, Sonny felt the weight of his mother's lack of partnership in many ways.

His life with Mom didn't seem out of bounds at the time. Like most mothers, she insisted that he do his homework and help her with chores. He wasn't naturally inclined to study or gifted at academics, but his application was rewarded with achievement. He participated in some student activities, but he rarely hung out with classmates after school. There was nothing extreme in his life that would indicate to people a troubled childhood. But trouble was growing unnoticed.

He was his mother's only friend. Even before the divorce, she would talk to him about her issues with his father. She seemed to be unaware of what is appropriate to share with a little boy. At six years old he didn't understand what she was saying, but he did understand that she was having trouble, his father was part of the problem, and somehow he, Sonny, was supposed to help. He knew that she liked him to keep her company. She didn't have friends or interests. She had a boring job. She complained to him about her boss and her good-for-nothing brother, his Uncle James. And especially, she complained about his father.

He came to understand that his main job was to feed his mother's spirits. It was difficult for him to justify going out, even on weekends. In the eleventh grade, he dated a girl once, taking her for a burger and a movie, only to come home to find his mother sitting in front of a turned-off TV, not having eaten, asking sadly if he had had a good time. He still dated a little, because it was expected by his peers, but it was a joyless business. He used homework and chores as an excuse to avoid it.

He went to college at the University of Michigan in Ann Arbor, so he could commute from home, and he stayed at Michigan for dental school. He got his own apartment when he began his dental practice, but many nights he still stayed in his old room in his mother's house.

A Place in His Heart

When a mother's emotional needs are satisfied only by her son, she will not be able to tolerate his natural separations. She will greet his efforts to venture outward with various forms of discouragement and disapproval. In some cases, this discouragement is blatant, but with Sonny it was more subtle. To a little boy, a lack of enthusiasm from his mother can be a strong message. Part of a mother's role is to encourage and tolerate healthy separation against the natural tendency of the child to cling. Further, she needs to see the value of the father in bonding with his son, because it is his father who will help him eventually to move out into the world. However, an enmeshed mother is not able to do this. Whatever she is thinking consciously, she *unconsciously* wants her little boy to stay home and take care of her.

A good childhood includes a natural, long process of weaning, where the son becomes more and more connected to others and less and less connected to his mother. A mother who allows her son to overattune to her needs at the cost of his own is setting up a lifetime of difficulties for him. A conscientious mother and an involved father may worry about how to guide this weaning process, realizing that good closeness at five may be bad closeness at ten. However, the boy will generally set his own pace of separation, if he is responding to his own needs and not his mother's.

The father is important here. He is the "bridge" for the son out of the early mother-son bond into manhood. In *Raising Boys: Why Boys Are Different—and How to Help Them Become Happy and Well-Balanced Men*, Steve Biddulph points out that the natural process of development for boys makes the mother primary in the boy's first five years, then the father between the ages of five and twelve, and then male mentors in adolescence. Inevitably, when I see mother-son enmeshment, there is a distant or absent father. One common story goes like this:

The father wants to escape from his wife and uses his son as a placating sacrifice: Take *him* and let *me* go. That this scenario is usually unconscious doesn't make it any less real. Or any less destructive.

The father and mother must form a bond with each other that keeps the son at an age-appropriate distance from his mother and leads over time to a young man with a yearning in his heart, knowing at least in his intuition that he must go out into the world to satisfy it. He will naturally find this quest exciting and joyful, even if challenging.

This was not the case for Sonny. He was "stuck" with his mother. He was going through the motions with Anne, but the joy was not there. In the depths of his heart, Sonny was unhappy and wanted freedom. But it was easier for him to let things stay unchanged. Guilt trumps desire. The price of freedom—disappointing his mother—was too much for him.

In the HBO TV series *The Sopranos,* the head gangster, Tony Soprano, is destructively enmeshed with his mother. She is a controlling, dominating force in his life. When he encounters her, he feels guilty and inadequate, belittled and diminished. Then he becomes frustrated and enraged. Frequently he

SYMPTOMS OF MEM:
Feeling Guilty and Inadequate

A MEM's inability to satisfy his mother makes him feel guilty. Whenever he has an encounter with his mother—either real or in his head, either as a child or later as an adult—his sense that he has inadequately served her is reinforced. Feeling excessive guilt and inadequacy is a key symptom of enmeshment.

is shown expressing the way he feels in violent acts, but with other people, not his mother. Although the conflict between Tony and his mother is exaggerated, it illustrates how a MEM will sometimes express his feelings of guilt and inadequacy through explosive anger at other people.

Anne Meets Dad and Mom

It was the third month of their relationship, and Anne was pleased when Sonny invited her to a family barbecue. Meeting the family seemed like progress.

Almost the first person they recognized after they arrived was Sonny's father.

"Hi, Dad," Sonny said. "This is Anne."

She smiled, looking radiant. His father returned the smile and took her in.

"The pleasure is all mine, honey," he said. He offered his hand, and she accepted it. He turned to Sonny without letting go of Anne. "I'm glad you're here, Sonny. Your mother's on the warpath again. Why don't you go over and take care of her, the way you do? I'll introduce Anne around for you."

Sonny, alone now, went to find his mother. She was sitting by herself, looking cross. She brightened when he came up.

"Hi, Mom," he said. "How's it going?"

"Let me tell you what your idiot uncle has done this time," she began. Sonny sighed and sat down.

Half an hour later, he managed to slip away. He joined Anne, who was talking passionately to a circle that had gathered around her. He enjoyed her arm coming around his waist, but he was worried. *I've got to get this over with*, he thought.

"Anne," he interrupted when he could. "I'd like you to meet Mom." She let him lead her away.

His mother was sitting in the same spot where he had left her. "This is Anne," he said. "You remember, the girl I've been dating."

His mother took her time, as if slow to recognize them together. "Hello, Anne," she said.

"Sonny has told me how close you two are," Anne said. "I think that's wonderful."

"Sonny knows how to take care of his mother," the elderly woman replied. She said no more.

Sonny shrank inside. He felt ashamed. He wanted to get away.

"We've got to go," he said, then turned and made Anne say good-bye over her shoulder.

They drove home in silence. He dropped her off and refused to come in. Later he wouldn't acknowledge to her that anything had happened. But he was more distant. He made excuses. He saw her less often.

Sonny Opens His Eyes

Often a MEM can't see that he can continue to have a relationship with his mother while beginning to develop an independent relationship with himself and then a relationship with someone else. He holds in his mind a rigid either/or viewpoint: "I either have to be with my mother, or I have to reject her. And I can't reject her, because I have too much guilt and I am terrified of feeling disloyal. I can't even think about it. You don't understand how bad it feels."

This is the core dilemma for a MEM. The inappropriate loyalty and devotion are intense. There's guilt and fear of retaliation connected to any attempt to separate. It becomes easier to stay put and live an ambivalent and compromised life.

SYMPTOMS OF MEM:
Commitment Phobia

At first, a MEM will be adoring, passionate, and enthusiastic, but one day without warning he will back away. As the connection turns into an opportunity to bond or commit, a MEM has a tendency to panic and want to escape. Even a small commitment—like a movie or a travel reservation—can seem overwhelmingly difficult.

I wanted to help Sonny get some perspective on his relationship with Anne. Could I help him see the bind that *she* was in, the fact that if she pressured him, he pulled away, but if she didn't pressure him, nothing would happen?

"Anne is overreacting," Sonny said to me. "I just haven't made up my mind. There are lots of wonderful women out there. How do I know Anne is the one?"

"What qualities does Anne lack, then?" I asked.

"I don't know."

"She's told you she won't wait forever," I persisted. "Do you understand why?"

"I guess so," he conceded. "Her biological clock is ticking. She wants children."

"Are you afraid of losing her?"

"I'm not sure."

"She thinks your relationship with your mother is a problem."

"Mom's not real enthusiastic about Anne," Sonny conceded.

"What Anne is really concerned about is your mother's control of your time. She can page you night and day, and you never say no to her."

"Well, what else can I do?" he said, sounding miserable.

"You can set boundaries with her," I said. "You can limit the circumstances when she is allowed to page you, for example."

He just looked at me and pulled at his beard.

Sonny was stuck, torn between his own wishes and his mother's pull. I couldn't tell him what to think. He needed to discover for himself that his dilemma wasn't about Anne but his own ambivalence. I was persistent in his therapy to help him see this, and in time he began to get the point.

*

"You know," he said to me one day, "I don't think my mother wants me to get married. She wouldn't like any girlfriend I had. She never liked my girlfriends, not even when I was a little kid. She wants me to take care of her for the rest of her life."

This was the critical moment of insight I had been waiting for. It was a first breaking of the hard ice of his denial.

"Do you know what you just said?" I asked him.

"No," he admitted, looking a little shocked at my excitement. "What did I say?"

"You said 'I don't think my mother would like any girlfriend I had. She doesn't want me to get married. She wants me to take care of her for the rest of her life.' How does it feel to say that?"

"It feels okay," he said, a little tentative. He grinned. "It feels scary," he admitted. "I don't want to hurt my mother."

"You're not hurting her. You're just talking to me."

"Still, I'm all she's got."

"You don't need to be constantly on call for her. She's not

decrepit. She doesn't have to be as dependent on you as she is now."

"Mom won't let me off that easy."

"This may come as a shock, Sonny, but you don't need her permission. That's what 'setting boundaries' is about. She will accept less of you. What choice has she got?"

"She'll be furious."

"Maybe so," I agreed.

"She'll sulk for months. She won't speak to me."

"When you were little, that was a catastrophe. But now it isn't. In fact, it will give you more time to be with Anne." He considered this and smiled, but it was a worried smile. "You know what, Sonny? Believe it or not, your mom can take care of herself. And she will if she has to."

He nodded, uncertain. I hoped he would think over what I'd just said.

✑

Soon after that Sonny reported to me about a phone call with his mother that had opened his eyes.

"Mom wanted me to come over to help her with something in the basement, and I said I could come on Saturday. It was difficult not to say 'I'll be right over,' but I did it. And guess what? She immediately began to cry and said I didn't care about her, now that I had a girlfriend. I was amazed. *Wow,* I thought. *She really does* want *to control my life. I never saw this before.* Just like you've been trying to tell me. She didn't miss a beat. I was not supposed to put her off, no matter what other plans I had."

"What are you feeling about the phone call?" I asked.

"I don't know. Of course, I still love my mother. But I got mad, and I think I'm still a little mad."

"Why are you angry?"

"She made me feel like I don't exist. That what I want doesn't matter."

"And that makes you feel angry?"

"Angry and sad," he admitted. "It made me feel lonely."

"Maybe you felt irrelevant or dismissed?"

"Yes," he said. "Irrelevant. Dismissed. That's exactly it."

*

One day Sonny came to see me and started to talk as soon as he got in the door.

"Remember the Labor Day party my uncle always has?"

"I think you mentioned that last year," I said.

"Right," he said. "Well, we went back last week, and it was amazing. My father comes up, and he says 'Why don't you go over and talk to your mother?' Just like that. Just like he did last year."

"Maybe he's done it all your life," I suggested.

"I guess so," he agreed. "But I never noticed it like this before. I was amazed, and I said 'No, I'm not going to do that. I've got Anne over here to talk to.' And he just looked at me for a minute, and then he walked away. He didn't like it! He didn't talk to me again the whole day."

"How did that feel to you?"

"I was okay with it. I went over and put my arm around Anne, and I felt completely fine. I said hello to my mom later, but I didn't let her rope me into listening to a long list of complaints. I wanted to relax and have a good time."

"I'm impressed," I said. And I was.

*

Finally Sonny faced the bitter task of setting boundaries with his mother. Of course, after all his therapy work, it turned out to be "easy." No catastrophes occurred. His mother grumbled and sulked. As he predicted, she refused to talk to him for a few months, but in the end she could do nothing but give in. He had to put up with her disappointment. It was a loss. He was no longer "golden" in her eyes. In return, he could actually plan a life with Anne, and they became engaged.

Sonny's mother never forgave Anne for taking her boy. They visit her once a month. The visits are rather strained. Sonny calls her once a week. He won't allow her to criticize Anne during the phone calls, which he limits to fifteen minutes. Other calls are taken by voice mail. Lonely and seeking other outlets, she has become active in her church and finds supportive acquaintances there.

∽

In the chapters to follow, we will consider how mother-son enmeshment looks for other men. For example, Doug was a womanizer; Tony could commit to his partner but to nothing else; Sam was a cybersex addict; and Father Mark had a problem with shoplifting, fooled around with his female parishioners, and had a food addiction. All were slaves to their unconscious ghosts, until therapy set them free.

2 DOUG'S FIRST DATE
The Womanizer

The floor in Doug's room was covered with discarded clothes. He had already spent half an hour trying to get everything just right. He wanted to look cool, but he didn't want anyone to guess that he cared about it.

His dad had taken him to get his driver's license that day and had given him permission to use the car for a date with Kathy. He had been looking forward to this day forever. A car. A girl. And no adults.

"Mom," he said, finding her in front of the TV. "Do I look okay?"

"You look fine, honey," she said without taking her eyes from the screen. "What are you worried about?" she added when he didn't go away.

"It's my first real date!"

Now she did look up. "I told you I don't like that girl," she said, bringing him into focus. "I don't think you should spend so much time with her."

"We're just going to Coney Island."

She turned to Doug's father. "Frank, help me out with this. Tell him you don't want him going out with that girl."

"Sweetie, she's a nice girl. Let the boy go. He just got his license. It's a special occasion."

"Right, Frank," she said, rolling her eyes. "You just like her short skirts. The girl's a slut. My son deserves better."

"Mom, it's none of your business. I'm going."

Doug moved to leave, but his mother jumped up and blocked his way.

"You're not going anywhere in that car."

"Dad said I could go." Doug turned to his father. "Dad? Isn't that right?"

But his father looked at his angry wife, gave his son an apologetic shrug, and shrank down in his chair.

"You're not going anywhere!" his mother repeated.

Doug stood looking at her, leaning forward a little and then back, as if he were considering pushing her away.

"You wouldn't dare take that car without our permission," she warned him.

Doug thought about it and decided she was right. He wouldn't dare, not without his father backing him up. Doug went upstairs. He called Kathy to say that he was having car trouble. Then he went back to his room and closed the door.

Can't Stop Screwing Around

Doug came to see me because he realized that he was about to start an affair with his boss's wife. He had done such things before, but this time he had doubts.

"She tells me 'I'm lonely. My husband's always staying late at work. I know you understand.' Just one little move from me. That's all it would take."

"It sounds like you don't want that to happen."

"I'm tired of getting nowhere," he said. "I'm forty-five. All my friends have families. I've dated a few good women, but somehow they just slipped away. I think I lost some opportunities there. Meanwhile, I've taken care of a lot of lonely wives. And what did I get for it?"

"What do you think?"

"It's pretty much adding up to nothing. But I still can't resist. Can you help me get out of this?"

"I don't know you, but I'm going to trust that your concern is valid. Can you make a commitment not to act out with your department head's wife while you and I try to sort out your story?"

"Okay, I guess so," he said. "What should I do?"

"Set boundaries with her. Tell her 'You're a nice person, but I'm starting to get uncomfortable listening to you talking about your husband, my friend and boss. Perhaps for your sake and mine, we should keep it casual.' That sort of thing."

"That sounds good," he agreed. Then he added, "These 'desperate housewives' come and go, but they're not really what I want. I want a wife of my own." He shrugged. "The women I date just never seem right after a while."

"Have you ever been married?"

"Once just after med school. It was a disaster. She was sweet until we got married, then she never stopped complaining. I got out of it without much damage."

"What kind of relationship did your parents have?"

"I don't think they had much of a connection."

"How did you and Mom get along?"

"Fine. She was lonely. I was lonely. She kept me company. I kept her company. That was a long time ago. I hardly see her anymore. My mother isn't my problem. My problem is all these women."

I understood at once that Doug's relationship with his mother most likely had a good deal to do with his current difficulties. But he wasn't aware of it. He wanted to change the subject, so I let him.

"You said you date a lot." I said. "Anybody special?"

"I've been dating Susan on and off for years. We like each other. Nothing serious."

"Do you think it might get serious?"

"It could, but it isn't."

"Would you mind giving up dating around?"

"Sure, I would," he admitted. "I like to date. It's just this other thing that's a problem. Kids. Family. That stuff."

Doug was smart, but he wasn't beyond fooling himself. He wanted me to help him make a commitment and have a family, but his "dating" was his emotional escape route. If I could help him make a commitment and have a family, and keep the escape route. . . . That's what he really wanted.

It took him a few sessions to admit that his "dating" was womanizing. Although he told himself he was looking for a wife, he went out with women half his age that he ran into at random and left without much thought.

Susan was different. He liked her, and their connection was more long term. But he kept "leaving her" to try someone new. He was vague on the nature of their relationship.

"What's Susan's point of view?" I asked him, after he had begun to trust me. "Does she think you two have an exclusive relationship? Does she know you date other women?"

"I don't lie about it," he said.

"If she were sitting with us right now"—I indicated an empty chair—"and I asked her, 'Are you and Doug dating exclusively?' what would she say?"

He shrugged.

"Do other people assume you and Susan are a couple?" I persisted.

"That reminds me of something," he said. "I was out last week with a cute girl from the hospital cafeteria. Beautiful legs. . . . Anyway, in comes my department head with his wife, and he says hello, and he calls her 'Susan.' I was embarrassed and so he got embarrassed. I went to correct him, and I got it wrong, too, so she had to correct me. It was a mess." Doug caught his breath. I waited.

"See, it's not really what I want anymore," he confessed. "I used to love people to see me with cute girls. Now, so what? And where's it going?"

"That's the main question," I agreed.

"I told you I got married right out of medical school. I thought if I was married I could settle down, stop wanting every woman who came along. But it didn't work. My wife was complaining all the time. She expected me to take care of her, and I could never get it right for her. I couldn't stay faithful. It didn't last even a year."

When Doug told me this, I could see his dilemma as a reflection of an intrusive relationship with his mother. The two key symptoms, his womanizing and his marriage to a needy woman, suggested a behavior pattern I've had a lot of experience with. His unconscious mind carried two conflicting versions of his mother: an enveloping sexual goddess and a damsel in distress. He married the acceptable part, the woman who needed help, to avoid the forbidden part, the seductress. He wanted to get away from the seductress, but he couldn't say no to her. His womanizing—chasing women and then dropping them—was his way of acting out this conflict. He captured the pleasure and avoided the entrapment. I decided to ask for more information.

"So you're afraid," I asked him, "that if you commit now, you'll end up with another needy woman who can't be satisfied and who won't satisfy you?"

"I guess so," he admitted.

"Is Susan like that?"

"Probably not. Susan's a friend, and she probably would be okay, but I just can't commit to her. I like variety. When I meet someone cute, I *have* to ask her out."

What Is Womanizing?

Peter Trachtenberg, in *The Casanova Complex,* makes the striking observation that womanizing hinges on abandonment. Both the womanizer and his women are aware of this, but not necessarily consciously. Part of the allure for the woman is the challenge of overcoming the promise of abandonment. *I'll be the one who keeps him,* she thinks. The womanizer is aware of this and exploits it. He knows she wants to be "the one," and he pretends he is offering her the chance.

For a woman who wants to be wary of womanizers, one rule is easy: Too much charm too soon is a red flag. It is the mask of the False Self, the sign of a manipulator. We will consider the False Self of MEM more fully in Chapter 8. Briefly, a MEM learned from his mother to play the role of solicitous attentive caretaker whose only need is to serve her. He learned to do this in opposition to his true feelings. He carries this "talent" into adulthood. He can ignore his True Self and use his False Self to charm and manipulate woman. See Figure 2.1.

The MEM is an effective seducer, because he is mostly un-

The False Promise of Prince Charming

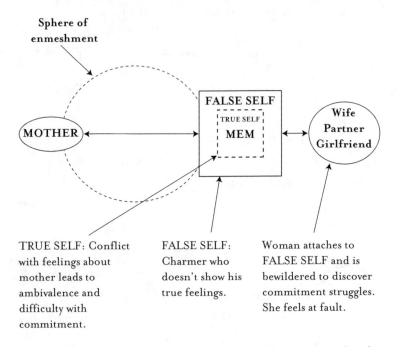

TRUE SELF: Conflict with feelings about mother leads to ambivalence and difficulty with commitment.

FALSE SELF: Charmer who doesn't show his true feelings.

Woman attaches to FALSE SELF and is bewildered to discover commitment struggles. She feels at fault.

Figure 2-1. The False Self contains the True Self and becomes a mask to face the world. The True Self is often suppressed, isolated, and detached. A MEM womanizer shows only his False Self, whose false promises eventually confuse and disappoint.

conscious of what he is doing. He will tend to believe in his False Self and be unaware of his True Self. He is "sincere." Some women find they have repeated affairs with womanizers. This is usually caused by their own unconscious templates. I recommend therapy for these women, so that they will have more options. I say more about this in Chapter 13.

Not all womanizers are the same. Some are calculating, remorseless, and utterly insensitive to the pain they cause. The MEM womanizer is usually different. He wants the sense of connection he gets from being with a woman, but he is unable to hold on to that sense. After all, he is commitment phobic. So he finds a woman to help him feel connected, and, when the feeling fades because of his commitment phobia, he goes to find another woman, so he can feel it again.

The MEM womanizer will be "in love" with a woman when he's with her, but later, when she is not there, he wants other women too. And late at night—those nights when he is alone—he is anxious about what kinds of obligations might be building. Then he feels his ambivalence and anger, his determination not to be trapped.

Womanizers want to be in control, and they hate the idea of being controlled. They think their ability to drop women proves their power. Ironically, they are controlled by their womanizing urges and impulses. Pursuing and abandoning is for them a compulsion, often a full-blown sexual addiction. When I point that out to them in my office, they look at me like I'm crazy, but in fact it is the case. Compulsions often begin as a way of controlling emotional pain, but over time, they lead to addictions and become their own problems.

SYMPTOMS OF MEM:
Addictions

Addictions can include working too much ("workaholism"), sexual addictions, eating disorders, financial disorders (hoarding or spending), and many others. The basic mechanism is the same for all addictions. An addiction begins as an attempt to dull the pain from some helpless time in childhood, what psychologists call "psychological trauma." A person can find escape, relief, and a sense of control in the addictive process.

"I'm not a womanizer," Doug said. "Well, maybe I am," he conceded. "I'd like to change my ways, I really would, but I just can't."

"So let's see if I can summarize," I said. "You feel in crisis. All your acquaintances are married, and they all have loving wives and cute children. In the meantime, you've been screwing around, and your encounters with overly needy women make you cautious about commitment."

Doug laughed, nodding. "That's it," he said.

Always with Mom, Never with Dad, and No Buddies

As a child, Doug was the object of his mother's passion and preoccupation. She doted on him. She took him with her to parties and events as her escort. She dressed him up in fancy, adultlike clothes. She taught him how he was to greet her friends and how he was to behave in adult company. He developed excruciatingly proper manners that were not moderated by peer pressure. Her friends were impressed; his friends didn't matter.

He told me about going to a concert with his mother when he was fourteen. As they waited in line, she had said to him in a loud stage whisper, "People think we're on a date. They think you're my boyfriend!" Doug had been proud. His mother was so beautiful.

Blocked from socializing by his mother's neediness and seductiveness, Doug lived much of his childhood without the company of peers. It left him with a residue of "not quite fitting in," which contributed to his low self-worth, a quality most people didn't see in him. However, it fed his workaholism by driving his need to prove himself.

SYMPTOMS OF MEM:
Low Self-Worth and Indecisiveness

Having been held back by his mother when he was a child, a MEM now holds himself back. He doesn't know what he wants, and he doesn't trust his own sense of what he likes. How is "low self-worth and indecisiveness" different from "feeling guilty and inadequate"? A MEM's low self-worth expresses itself as not trusting his own judgment, which is the cause of his indecisiveness. It's not a question of feeling guilty; he just doesn't know what to do. A MEM's sense of guilt comes from feeling bad about disappointing Mom. His guilt makes him feel inadequate, because he couldn't make her happy.

Over time, Doug's mother became jealous of him to the point that she didn't want to share him with his father. His father had wanted to spend time with him, but his mother had been too strong-willed and his father's determination too ineffective. Eventually, his father withdrew from the family, moving on to alcohol and occasionally other women. He was not there for Doug to help him fend off the enmeshment with his mother.

A Womanizing Workaholic Gets His Start

When he had first gone to college, Doug had been socially awkward. His mother had been his only "girlfriend." This had left him inexperienced. His first few movie dates in college were nice but nothing special. The special relationship in his freshman year was with his best buddy, John. They had gone to the same high school but had hardly known each other there. In college, however, they became inseparable pals. Doug got to experience for the first time what it meant to have a friend who wasn't his mother.

When Brenda, John's girlfriend, walked into Doug's room wearing just her slip, it wasn't that big a deal. Things were pretty casual around the dorm, and the girls often "invaded" the boys' floor to tease. But she had something in mind. She sat on his bed, crossed her legs, and said, "I love John, but I want you." She paused to let him take this in, then went on. "This will just be our little fun secret," she said, leaning over to kiss him. That was awkward, so she sat on his lap. "I can't do this with him," she confided, "because he wouldn't respect me in the morning, but with you it doesn't matter."

It was a catalytic moment for Doug. He had always been afraid of sexy girls, but what had he been so worried about?

The fun with Brenda lasted only a few weeks. John found out, and Doug lost his first buddy. It didn't occur to him to worry about that loss or grieve it; his training as a MEM had taught him that only women are important. Brenda wouldn't see him anymore, but it was easy to move on.

Brenda had uncorked the bottle that held Doug's genie, but his mother had put the genie in the bottle in the first place. Brenda's seduction was an explicitly sexual reenactment of the implicit seduction by his mother. The template had been established in his unconscious when he was five years old. It was activated by Brenda, somebody else's woman who wanted him, just as his mother had been his father's woman but wanted him. Like the perfectly correct alignment of the tumblers in a lock, this key combination of factors—seduction by a woman who belonged to another man—"clicked" for Doug and turned on the mechanism of his womanizing. From that moment, his unconscious would cause him to repeat and repeat this pattern of seducing another man's woman.

Doug hadn't realized how successful he could be with girls until he got away from his mother. By the end of his twentieth year, his sexual drive, his ability to please women, and his need to avoid the entrapment of female smothering reached their stable equilibrium.

✑

Doug didn't think he had a problem related to his mother when he came to see me. There *had been* a problem when he was younger, Doug admitted, but he didn't have a problem with her now. Doug's anger at his mother had evolved into disengagement. He grudgingly called her on Christmas and on her birthday, but he hated doing it. She was far away, living in Florida, and he thought he was essentially done with her. The opposite was true. He had never emotionally or sexually separated from her, and he was living his life trying to counter her influence. One of the long-term goals of his therapy would be to have him feel the depth and significance of his enmeshment.

Doug's father was still alive, although divorced from his mother. When Doug came to see me, his father was just as uninvolved with his son as ever. Doug's lifelong estrangement from his father was one of the influences that prevented him from seeking support from men. It didn't occur to him in college to say to himself, "I can't have sex with my best friend's girlfriend, because I value my buddy. I'm not going to do that to him. I don't want to lose him." His enmeshment with his mother set him up to be in competition with his father and, in later life, with all men. His womanizing not only let him play out his relationship with his mother, but it also allowed him to keep "besting" his father: "See, I can outdo you. I can take your woman away from you."

I'm Fine Now

Doug was pleased with himself. ". . . so then I said, just like you suggested, 'Susan, when you say that, I start feeling some resentment and I'd like to talk about it.' And she listened to me. It was great. It was such a relief. I felt so powerful, I wasn't even worried if she got mad. And guess what? She didn't get mad, and she listened to me. And *that* was such a relief. And you know what? I'll bet this will be the end of my ambivalence. It's a real breakthrough."

"That's great, Doug," I said, but I could sense what was coming, because it often does after about half a year of therapy with MEM.

"I've been seeing you now for six months," he went on, "and I've made a lot of progress. I'm really busy. I think maybe we could change my appointments to just once every other week. See how it goes."

"The usual reason people want to moderate their therapy," I told him, "is because they're up against something that's difficult to confront. You're naturally going to want to go the other direction from what you're uncomfortable with. We all do that. The problem is, if you back off now, you won't make any lasting changes. Five years from now, at the age of fifty, you'll be coming into my office saying 'I still can't commit.' Is it possible I'm right . . . you'll be in this same place five years from now?" It was an accurate projection, and he knew it.

"Let's give it another six months," I said, "and reevaluate then. Can you continue for six months?"

And so, reluctantly, fearfully, he agreed.

What Doug had presented to me was, "I need to cut back on my therapy. I'm better. I don't have time." But deep down his unconscious was saying, "If I keep coming here weekly, I'm going to get trapped. I'm not going to get out of this therapy relationship." That was his major fear in all relationships. "I can't get obligated to this therapist. I'll be giving him money forever. I'll never get out. I'll be trapped. I will no longer have a say." He was defending against the loss of his identity. He didn't consciously see that. All he saw was, "I'm busy. I'm feeling uncomfortable. I'm getting tired of driving across town every week. This is too much hassle."

He was having the same reaction to me that he had with his girlfriends, the echo of his trapped feelings as a little boy with his mother. The voice of his unconscious was whispering, "That happened with *your mother*. Don't let it happen with *him*."

Sober, Honest, and Facing His Past

Into his second year of therapy, Doug began to trust me at a deeper level. He was no longer just *complying* with therapy. He was participating out of his own desire to make his life better. He accomplished three things that year, all linked to one another. He let go of his womanizing; he acknowledged the significance of, and worked on, his issues with his mother; and he got honest with Susan.

I helped him look at his pattern of womanizing as a type of sexual addiction. Attracting women and then leaving them had seemed powerful to him, but he came to see he'd been holding himself hostage to his addiction. His womanizing was not about connecting and committing but rather about acting out the pain of his past and escaping the trap of enmeshment.

At the same time, we worked on getting Doug in touch with what happened in his childhood that powered his compulsive behavior. I had him confront his three core destructive beliefs about himself: (1) I am responsible for taking care of my mother; (2) my needs don't matter; and (3) being close to someone means being engulfed and controlled.

While Doug was letting go of womanizing and confronting his childhood, he needed to get honest with Susan, his favorite "date." He needed to get past the deluded "I didn't promise her anything" and to become scrupulously honest in a way his old manipulative self could never have imagined. Of course, he was still ambivalent, so he had to share that uncertainty with her.

He met with her in my office. "I've got some issues to work out in therapy," he told her. "I'm going to stop dating other women. But you're different. You're a friend, and maybe one day we can be more than friends to each other. But for now I've got to keep our relationship a little distant. I'm not assuming you'll wait for me. But if you want to wait, now you know what's going on."

Susan was confused and shocked. As far as she had known, she was his special woman, not so much from anything he said but by the way he had treated her. Now he was telling her that he had been repeatedly "unfaithful," and he wasn't sure about her after all.

"What I recommend to women in your situation," I told her, "is that you take your own 'time-out.' Don't give Doug any commitment while he's working on his issues. You obviously like each other. Maybe in the future you could consider a new relationship."

She nodded. It was a noncommittal response, but I sensed she understood me.

This session was a turning point for Doug. He wasn't keeping secrets anymore. He had been willing to explore and reveal the false sense of commitment between him and Susan, and he had been willing to give it up.

As we continued to work together, Doug stuck with his decision to give up his old life. He was now willing to journey into the underworld of his childhood and return with the contents of his own identity. He became more aware of his compulsive behaviors—workaholism and womanizing—as he learned to confront them. This type of journey is more an intuitive unfolding than a set of facts to learn. Just knowing "the facts" is never sufficient. He had to "feel" the need for change. In his new intuitive understanding, he became self-motivating. As we entered his third year of therapy, my role shifted to helping him interpret experiences, keeping him on track, and dealing with setbacks.

He was learning to take responsibility for his own choices. He began to understand commitment as freeing rather than confining. Living under the dominance of his mother had given him the habit of not taking responsibility for his choices and of not accepting them as his own. It created a kind of emotional detachment, a sense of unreality in him for the consequences of his behavior toward others.

He began to date again, but with a completely new program. He took things more slowly. He didn't feel compelled to obligate himself to a new woman, to win her over and best his father. He was less focused on controlling the situation. He had let go of seduction and conquest. He was no longer using women to satisfy an unsatisfiable need. He was finally "courting."

He couldn't help worrying if the new Doug—who wanted to go slow and not play a role—would still be attractive to women. I assured him that the women who were disappointed with the new Doug had their own issues, and it was better to let those women go. He asked Susan out, and they began to see each other again.

Mommy Doesn't Live Here Anymore

Today, Doug is a little freer to visit his mother, because now he is his own man. He's had his breakthrough, and he doesn't need to confront her about the past. He did need to establish boundaries to limit her intruding behavior. (Chapter 11 describes how to set limits with parents.) He visits her on his own terms. He stays in a motel. He comes by for a holiday or two. He doesn't spend a lot of time with her, because she's still very dysfunctional and tries to draw him into her private dramas. He wants to have some contact with her, but not very much. He can now extend some caring, and that's another breakthrough for him. The emergence of empathy for his mother could not have occurred while he was still so hurt and angry. After reaching this level of reconciliation with his mother, he is able to be more empathic toward all the women in his life.

Doug contacted his father. He discovered a sad drunk, gone to dementia and living in a nursing home, who hardly remembered he had a son. This was difficult for Doug. He had had hopes for some kind of reconciliation. However, his father had a lucid moment during Doug's visit, and Doug was able to tell him, "I no longer accept my mother's version of you." His father grasped and held his hand. Doug felt the spark of connection he had so desperately longed for. The father-son relationship had been interfered with by his enmeshment, but for this one moment Doug felt the love for his father he thought he had lost.

After all this psychological housecleaning, Doug was ready to settle down. And he liked Susan. His feelings for her hadn't gone away, and Susan was still available. He asked her to do joint therapy with him for a short time, because there were some issues that still bothered him. Also, he wanted the two of them to learn to communicate better as a couple. I saw them once and then referred them to a couples counselor. As Doug was ending his work with me, he proudly told me they had become engaged.

Fight Compulsions with a Life of Meaning

Doug's urge to womanize when he feels stressed is an issue that will resurface. Such a well-grooved pattern doesn't just go away. Like the alcoholic who is always an alcoholic, no matter how long he has been sober, Doug may always have a lingering eye for other women. It is part of his unconscious template. It can be managed but not completely eliminated. That said, he doesn't have to go back to his womanizing ways.

I counseled him to be aware of what stressors and disappointments trigger his compulsion. For example, he may sometimes feel unhappy and trapped by the burdens and responsibilities of being a husband and father. He's going to want relief. He's going to want to leave, and leaving for Doug is womanizing.

I suggested that he find healthy ways to escape, such as a hobby he can keep separate from his marriage and family. Having innocent forms of release will make his womanizing urge less intense. I suggested he develop some male friends. I also suggested he make some conscious decisions around values. Leading a life of meaning, fulfillment, and balance is the best antidote to compulsions. Eventually, a recovering MEM learns how to commit to some kind of meaning beyond himself, and he comes to understand that committing need not be entrapping.

I invited Doug to return to therapy if he found himself slipping back into his old destructive habits and beliefs. If he acted out again, he would be returning to the grief of his past life. He would be putting in jeopardy the benefits of his hard-won committed relationship.

❧

Many of my MEM clients have trouble committing to a woman, but for some, commitment phobia is expressed as irresponsibility and immaturity. Such was the case with Tony, who had trouble committing to everything *except* his girlfriend, Elizabeth. Her concern and confusion brought her to my office, as I describe in the next chapter.

3 TONY JUST WANTS TO HAVE FUN
The Perpetual Adolescent

Elizabeth was desperate.

"This is important, Tony," she said.

"Yeah? What's up?"

"My mother's flying in tomorrow. She'll be here around five-thirty, but I'll be in Toledo until six. I'm doing a workshop for the social workers. I can't meet her until seven."

"You want me to pick her up? I've got a lot to do tomorrow. Can't she take the limo?"

"I can't afford the limo. And she gets very confused in airports. She wouldn't even be able to find the limo."

"What about Rachael?"

"Her car is in the shop. She can't do it."

"And I guess Mary Ann won't help a friend in need?"

"I left her a message. She hasn't gotten back to me."

"It figures."

"Look, Tony. Why can't you just commit to giving me some help?"

"Well, if you're going to make a federal case out of it, I guess I'll do it."

"You're sure?"

"I'll be there. Say . . . why don't we get some pizzas, invite some people, and make it a party?"

"That sounds like fun," Elizabeth said. "But I'll be very busy with the workshop, so I won't be able to call to remind you."

"Don't give it another thought. While she's here, why don't we tell her we've decided to get married?"

"Because we haven't. I'm not sure you're ready for that."

"What do you mean? Of course I'm ready."

"I mean, kids are a lot of work."

"I love kids. I'll take them out on my boat. I'll teach them how to Jet Ski."

"Okay. One thing at a time. About my mother . . ."

"No problem. It's covered."

❦

The next day, as Elizabeth was stuck in traffic heading north from Toledo, her cell phone went off. It was her mother. No one had met her. She didn't know what to do. She was frightened. Elizabeth couldn't believe it. She just couldn't believe it. She called Tony.

"Yeah," he said. "Elizabeth? Oh, my God. Your mother! You know, I was cleaning my snowmobile, and I just lost track of time. I'll go over now."

"It's too late now. I can get there as fast as you can. And she's having a panic attack. You know how she is!"

There was a pause on the line. "Damn" was all Tony could think to say. Elizabeth hung up on him, shaking with fury and frustration. She wiped the sweat off her face, along with a few tears. She felt so let down. She couldn't take this anymore.

He's a Little Defiant, and He Has Lots of Toys

Elizabeth told me she wanted to talk about her boyfriend.

"He wants to marry me, but all he ever thinks about is playing. He's lovable, but I don't think I could trust him to be a good partner."

"Tell me more."

"Well, for instance, he leaves work early to go to a ball game or take out his boat. I'm surprised they don't fire him. He does finance stuff for some auto company. I guess it doesn't interest him very much.

"I'd support him if he wanted to look for a better job. It's just that he doesn't seem to be serious about working at all. What if we marry and have a couple of kids and then he gets fired?

"He got an inheritance a few years ago, a pretty good amount of money. He quit his job, and he just went crazy buying things and having a good time.

"He loves to buy stuff. Grown-up toys, like the latest computer, with the fastest processor and the biggest screen. He got a boat, and then he didn't have any place to keep it, so he bought this old farm just because it was on a lake. Then he got a Jet Ski, then a snowmobile, then another Jet Ski. Of course, he had to get a Corvette and a Hummer. He didn't save a penny, and I begged him to."

"Where did this inheritance come from?"

"Oh, his mother," Elizabeth said. "He was devoted to her."

"What kind of job do you think he'd be interested in?"

"I think he should have been an architect. It's what he wanted to do, before his mother got him to go business school. He still draws pictures of houses when he's doodling. He can't help it. He lights up when he points out a building he especially likes."

"You don't think it's too late?"

"He could go back to college. But I don't think he will."

"So money is your main concern?"

"Actually, it's not. It's that he's so unreliable." She looked sad. "He really let me down last week." She told me about her mother and the airport. "I thought he would pull himself together, if I really needed him. It shocked me that he didn't. My father was like that. Mother had to remind him if he was supposed to do something, and she had to remind him exactly when it needed to be done, because otherwise he would forget."

"What's Tony like as a person?"

"He's a little defiant. He wore tennis shoes with his tuxedo to the prom in high school to make a statement."

"You went to high school together?"

"No, but he's told me that story about a hundred times. So tell me, Dr. Adams, what should I do? Should I marry him or not? It's driving me crazy."

"It sounds like you're trying to figure out if marrying Tony would create a situation for you like the one you grew up with. The best thing would be for me to meet with both of you. Do you think he would do that?"

"I'll ask him," she said.

What's the Problem?

Tony had agreed to come to a session with Elizabeth, but, when the time came, he didn't show up.

"It's my fault," Elizabeth said. "I should have gone and gotten him."

"He may come in late," I suggested. "In the meantime, you said that Tony was devoted to his mother?"

"She was a successful businesswoman. I didn't particularly

like her, and she certainly didn't like me, but I have to admit she made that business work, when most businesses around here were failing. She started her own PR firm, began with nothing, ended up with over a dozen employees. Tony was proud of her, and I don't blame him."

"But you two didn't get along?"

"Tony would call her every day or go see her. He took me along sometimes. She would just ignore me, pretend I wasn't there. If I tried to say something, she would somehow turn my comment into a 'joke'—you know, be sarcastic. Tony said she was that way with everybody, but I don't know."

"How did she get along with Tony?"

"He catered to her. He would do whatever she asked him to. He always agreed with her, no matter how ridiculous her opinions were."

"Was Tony also close to his father?"

"I don't think so. When Tony was a child, his father traveled a lot for his job. Tony said he wasn't around much."

"And his mother has passed away?"

"Yes, and I was hoping he would become more focused after she died. But he's pretty much the same."

"Before she passed away, though, you say he called her every day?"

"Tony was crazy about his mother. He asked her advice about everything."

Tony walked in on us just then.

"Sorry I'm late," he said. "Traffic was nasty. Hi, Liz." He sat beside her on the couch and took her hand. "What did I miss?"

"We were talking about your mother," Elizabeth said.

"Oh, yeah," he said. "She could kick ass, couldn't she, Liz?"

"Elizabeth says you were very close to your mother."

"My best friend in all the world," he agreed.

"Did Elizabeth talk with you about why she came to see me?"

He looked at her. "Did you?"

"Yes, I did," she said. "I want to see if you can get serious about us. I want to know if it makes sense to marry you."

"I don't see what the problem is," he said. "We had a good time just last weekend. Ed was there. We had some drinks on the boat. Ed and I had fun with the Jet Skis. You took a swim."

"I'm afraid you're going to lose your job, the way you goof off. I've begged you a million times to find something you really want to do."

"I'd rather goof off."

"They're going to fire you."

"They don't fire anybody. Plenty of people goof off more than me."

"You're not lazy. You're always doing something. You spend hours tinkering with your boat. Why can't you put the same energy into something serious?"

Tony shrugged. "I'm doing okay."

Elizabeth turned to me. "How do I make him want to grow up?"

"Sometimes a person will try to cover childhood wounds by seeking distractions," I said.

I decided I might as well go on. I explained about mother-son enmeshment and how it could lead to a lack of direction, initiative, and responsibility. Elizabeth was nodding, interested. Tony didn't seem to be listening. I tried to focus on what would be most relevant to him.

"Some MEM are perpetual adolescents," I said. "Their commitment phobia comes out as an aversion to responsibility. This kind of MEM resists making any kind of commitment, even a trivial commitment, like meeting for lunch or a movie. He doesn't want to be 'boxed in' by making promises. 'I'll get there when I get there' is his motto.

"His connection to his partner may be sweet and sincere, he may be faithful and affectionate, but he generally is in no hurry to develop the potential of the relationship."

"That's on target," Elizabeth said. She looked to Tony, but he seemed to be thinking about something else.

"Another characteristic of the perpetually adolescent MEM," I went on, "aside from chronic lateness, is that his heart isn't in his work. He may be a 'success' in his career, but he's still just going through the motions."

I paused to think about how to frame this. Why *does* the perpetually adolescent MEM, like Tony, hold back from pursuing his heart's desire?

"What this MEM is doing," I said, "is resisting being controlled. He avoids serious pursuits, because they feel confining."

"Doesn't that sound right, Tony?" Elizabeth said, "The way you decided not to go to architecture school."

"I'm not so sure. Mom straightened me out on that. I'd never have made it."

"It seems you try to stay as free as possible by being as uncommitted as possible," I told him. "I admire you for having the spirit to resist being controlled. But can you see that you're hurting yourself? Your resistance is sabotaging your ability to know what you love and to pursue it with full energy."

Elizabeth was nodding, agreeing with me.

Tony shrugged. "You know, that's pretty deep stuff, but I'm doing okay. I'm having fun. Maybe you should try it."

The Flying Boy

They arrived together for the next session. I wanted to start them off in a lighter vein, so I asked how they had met. Tony turned to Elizabeth.

"I met Tony when I was just out of college," she said. "He was part of a fun group of friends, and he shared them with me. There was a time when the whole bunch was meeting every night. It was a never-ending party.

"And Tony was always the life of that party. He brought the dope, or maybe it would be beer. He has this crazy fun sense of humor. He can tell the most outrageous jokes." She paused and smiled, looking over at him. Then she lost the smile.

"But now that's over. Everybody's married, got responsibilities, moved to the suburbs. There's just one of Tony's old buddies he still sees."

"Ed," Tony offered.

"That's right," Elizabeth said. "Ed was married, but it didn't work out. Tony's married friends can't put up with his unreliability. Tony was forty-five minutes late for lunch with one of them. Of course, the man wasn't there when Tony showed up."

"What do you think, Tony?" I asked him.

He shrugged. "People come. People go. We still have a good time."

"It didn't matter when we were single and just hanging out," Elizabeth said. "But now . . . if I did agree to marry you, I wonder how late you'd be to the wedding."

"That's one party I'd be early for," Tony assured her.

"In spite of your frustrations," I said to her, "you and Tony have been together for years."

"Yes," she said, and her expression softened. "He was so sweet. He actually proposed on our second date."

"I can see you really like each other, but still . . . Elizabeth, you came to see me because you were concerned. How do you envision things getting better?"

"I want a husband and a family," she said. "I'm tired of just fooling around."

"Tony's eager to marry you. He'd have a family with you."

"That's true. But I don't want to have to take care of *him* while I'm taking care of the children."

"I guess that's the issue, isn't it?" I said. "What do you think, Tony?"

He shrugged. "I love children. I got the boat. I thought you liked going out on the boat. The kids will love it too. In the winter I'll teach them how to snowmobile."

"Why won't you get the point?" Elizabeth said, flaring a little.

He just shrugged.

"It may be more that he *can't* get the point." I said. "The therapist John Lee described men who won't accept adult responsibilities, who remain as self-absorbed and unreliable as teenagers, in his book *The Flying Boy*. I've always appreciated the image of these 'flying boys' soaring away from responsibilities. Perpetual adolescents are often viewed with contempt or anger, as they fly away whenever they're needed to help out. But they're the way they are because they've been wounded, and criticism doesn't help them get better. Tony isn't willfully refusing to grow up. He's stuck in his adolescence, and he can't see any safe alternative. But there are ways to help him."

Elizabeth wanted to hear more, so I talked with them about approaches to healing, as discussed in this book.

Whatever Happens Happens

The next time they came to see me, Elizabeth wanted to talk about mother-son enmeshment. She had absorbed the information I'd provided in the previous sessions, read some of the books I recommend on the subject, and was excited by her new insights. She eagerly explained everything to Tony, looking to me for confirmation every few sentences. She had done her homework, but I was concerned that she might be overwhelming Tony. I intervened as soon as I could.

"Tony, you've been very patient here, listening to Elizabeth," I said. "She thinks your mother was sometimes intrusive. What do you think?"

He was slouching, and he looked defensive. "Mom was sometimes a pain," he admitted. "But so what? I loved her, and she loved me. She did everything she could for me. I might not be much of a businessman, but that's not her fault. She was a wonderful woman. Anyway, I'm doing okay."

Elizabeth was gaping at him.

"What?" he said to her. "Don't look at me like that. You think I'm not the right man for you? Okay. That's okay with me, you know? We've been together for a long time, but okay . . . Whatever happens happens, you know? I mean, if that's what you've got to do . . . it's okay with me." He shrugged.

Tony's reaction didn't surprise me. He wasn't ready to look at himself. He had spent his life flying away from the difficult work of being a responsible adult. It wasn't a shock that he would avoid the much more difficult work of examining his own behavior or his relationship with his mother.

And Now *This?*

Neither Elizabeth nor Tony wanted to start talking the next time they came to see me. I decided to see if Tony would be able to respond to Elizabeth's new perspective.

"Suppose for the sake of argument that your relationship with your mother did happen to be an issue for you on some level," I said to him. "Stay with me on this, Tony," I added, since he seemed to be drifting. "If it is true, and Elizabeth's observations about your mother and your family have some validity, would you be willing to do some therapy that would help make some changes?"

He just looked at me.

"Would you be willing to consider doing something like that, if it might keep Elizabeth around?"

"I don't get this, you know," he replied. "We're having good times for years and all of a sudden now *this?* You know, I love kids. I'm a good guy. We've had a lot of fun. . . ."

I looked over at Elizabeth. Her face had changed. It had taken on a firmness. It had become hard. Neither of them wanted to talk more, and we ended the session early.

A Lifetime of Pain

The next time I saw them, Elizabeth came in with something she had prepared to say.

"I love you, Tony," she began. "I care about you. But I can't marry a man who won't take his responsibilities seriously. I can't live with that for the rest of my life. I've made a decision. I'm going to bow out of this." She began crying, but went on. "I care for you. I love you. But you will never change, and, if we marry, we will have a lifetime of pain. I've got to save us both from that." Then she just sat and cried.

I passed her the Kleenex box. I looked over to see how Tony was responding. He looked blank. Then he said, "That's too bad," and shrugged.

Elizabeth was calmer now. She thanked me for my efforts, stood, and was gone. Tony still sat and stared.

"What's going on for you?" I asked.

"I guess I'll go too," he said, and stood.

"You can still work on this," I said. "Your issues aren't going to just go away. You can. . . ."

But by then I was talking to myself.

He Won't Be Controlled

Mother-son enmeshment can rob a man of his ability to initiate. We see this in Tony. He was committed to his partner—in the sense of being loyal and faithful, although not in the sense of being reliable—but he couldn't commit to anything else. His chronic lateness was an easy-to-see indicator of this.

WHY ARE PERPETUALLY ADOLESCENT MEM UNRELIABLE?

A perpetually adolescent MEM's unreliability is his way of saying no to being controlled by his mother. He often feels that a commitment to do a particular thing at a particular time is a trap he must escape from. Being late or "forgetting" is his way of saying "You can't control me."

↬

Consider the perpetually adolescent MEM's dilemma. The Disloyalty Bind is a powerful controlling force. He resists being controlled, but he still can't free himself from it. Caught between the Disloyalty Bind and his own desires, he finds compromise in play. But he loses his ability to pursue serious adult activities.

Anything that evokes control—like having to be on time—brings up his suppressed feelings of engulfment. However, he doesn't experience it that way. What he is aware of consciously is that commitments are burdensome and get in the way of his fun. The perpetually adolescent MEM expects always to be having a good time.

Adolescence and Individuation

Adolescence is a period of self-discovery, typically beginning at puberty and continuing into the early twenties. By the end of adolescence, if all goes well, a person will know what he (or she) believes and what he (or she) likes.

If all does not go well, there are two possible outcomes. Both are common for MEM. One is a continuation of adolescence. Tony illustrates this case. Here the MEM cannot achieve true adult intimacy with a partner. Not knowing who he is, he is restless and doesn't want to "settle down" to adult responsibilities. Even though he wants to marry Elizabeth, he has not accepted his need to change.

The other possible outcome is that the MEM pretends that he has discovered himself when he really hasn't. This pretender takes on a set of opinions, likes, and dislikes without actually feeling anything about them. For example, he might take on the views of his parents without actually knowing whether he believes these views or not. Typically, he holds his beliefs rigidly and sees the world in blacks and whites without any grays. He doesn't do well with the natural ambiguity of life.

Psychologists describe a person as "individuated" if that

person has successfully completed adolescence, ending the period of questioning with a clear sense of his or her own views and preferences. An individuated man has separated from his parents, so that he is now a distinct individual. A MEM is typically not individuated, because he is enmeshed with his mother. His identity has been lost in serving her needs. Researcher Erik Erikson clarified individuation in childhood development, which is explained by John and Linda Friel in their book *Adult Children*.

One important outcome of a man being individuated is that he can be in a committed relationship. If he is not individuated, he may date, he may marry, but he can't successfully and comfortably commit and settle down. He is always dissatisfied. This is more obvious for the perpetual adolescent than the pretender, but it is true of both. That is why the marriages that seem most solid can end with the man running away with his secretary or his student, shocking everyone because he is the *last* man in the world you'd expect it of. He was a pretender; his solid marriage was a pretense. He wasn't real, and it wasn't real.

MEM struggle to commit for two main reasons: (1) they're loyal to their mothers, and (2) they are not sufficiently individuated.

A Loving Rejection

About a year after I had last seen Tony and Elizabeth, Tony called me.

"How are you doing?" I asked him.

"Say, Doc," he said. "I think I missed an opportunity there. She was trying to tell me something. I didn't get it, so I didn't get her. I could kick myself for that."

"I'm hearing some regret," I said.

"Yeah," he agreed. "It's been eating me up. I didn't think it was that big a deal, but it really got to me, you know? I've been a basket case."

"That's too bad," I said. "It sounds like you'd like to talk it over." We made the appointment.

⌒

I knew this was a new Tony when he showed up on time.

"You know," he said, "Ed remarried. They had a baby. That's the last I've seen of him."

"Sounds like you miss his company," I said.

"See, I went out on the boat by myself. Big mistake! I had time to think, you know? I was so lonely, and I hadn't realized how much I would miss her."

"What did you think?"

"I don't know what I was thinking. We were together so long, I forgot what it was like to be alone. And everybody else is out of the picture. Even Ed."

"So, you're feeling some grief. These different events have caused you to think about your life."

"I really blew it, didn't I?"

"I admire you for feeling your grief and wanting to do something about it. I respect that."

"Really? Well, thanks."

"It seems like this hit you hard. Your losses: Elizabeth, Ed, your other friends."

"I didn't think I actually needed therapy, but okay, here I am. I'm willing to give it a try. That mother stuff. It began to make sense, you know?"

"What makes you say that?"

"I found an e-mail from Mom. I've actually kept all her e-mails. I reread a bunch of them. This one was after I broke up with the girl before Elizabeth. It was weird."

"What do you mean?"

"Mom was 'so delighted to have me back.' That's what she said. 'Delighted to have me back.' I just never thought about how weird that was. She was always saying stuff like that."

"I guess we should talk about it," I said, and we did.

***

Tony made good progress and was exceptionally motivated. His regret and sense of loss gave him insight as well as motivation. We spent most of our time together on his enmeshment issues. He also dealt with his disappointment and sadness at the loss of Elizabeth. He eventually began to understand how many of his life choices had been in rebellion against his mother. After that, the enmeshment began to loosen its grip on his behavior.

He sold his boat and decided to save some money. He still likes to play, but he has decided not to live to play. He's hoping the next time he meets somebody special, he'll be better prepared to appreciate her.

The last time he talked to me about his sense of loss around Elizabeth, he had a new feeling and a new insight. He was grateful that she had left. Her leaving was best for both of them. Without the shock of losing her, he never would have gotten clear.

He had come to me ready to begin his therapeutic journey. He worked on it for several years and then moved on. Last I heard, he was in architecture school.

Grief Can Lead to Growth

Before Tony turned his life around, the natural flow of his life force had been restricted and diverted by his enmeshment. He could not validate his own authentic self by following his passion for architecture. Instead, his passion had been split off from meaningful endeavors and restricted to playing. He had not attained his emancipated manhood. He remained undeveloped and immature, a perpetual adolescent.

When Elizabeth left Tony, he was shocked, missed her, then felt regret for letting her go. Some of the moments of deepest grief for my clients have been moments of regret and loss. But these moments of grief have often become opportunities for growth, as deep feelings uncover deep insights and insights can be energized into better choices.

❧

In the next chapter, we meet Father Mark, the apparent opposite of fun-loving, self-absorbed Tony. Father Mark was a Catholic priest who devoted himself and his life to serving others. He had convinced himself that his personal desires were gone and that he was free to dedicate himself to his parishioners. He had an iron will, but over time, something happened: Mark, the lonely human being, emerged from Father Mark, the selfless caretaker, and lonely Mark was demanding his due share of the world's bounty.

4 FATHER MARK IS KILLING HIMSELF
The Burned-out Caretaker

Father Mark took the two shoplifted CD sets from under his cassock and considered them. Woody Guthrie had always been his hero, and Pete Seeger could still bring tears to his eyes. Theirs were songs of the human spirit: "Hard Times," "This Land Is Your Land," "Turn, Turn, Turn." . . .

There was a knock at the office door.

"Just a minute," he shouted, as he put the stolen CDs away. It was Connie. He gave her his big, teddy-bear hug.

She sat on his old sofa, blushed, and tugged at her skirt. "I'm afraid I have a lot to confess, Father," she said.

"I'm ready to hear you, Connie."

"But come sit by me," she said. "You seem so distant." She patted the spot by her. "I've got so much to tell you."

So Father Mark sat where she indicated. She reached for his hand. He pulled back, but then she looked so hurt, he relented and let her hold his hand. When she began to kiss him, he let her do that too. Who was he to refuse to give her comfort? Then she wanted more than kissing, and he wasn't going to stop her. He wanted it too much to hold either of them back.

After Connie left, Father Mark felt both delight and shame. He took out a piece of paper and wrote his dead mother a letter.

"Dearest Mother," he wrote. "I miss you every day. I keep trying to get word of Katherine. Some people in the shelters think they saw her last winter. They say she was heading back to Chicago. I know she wishes she had come back to see you before you got sick. Sometimes when a person gets on the wrong path and they want to come back, they just don't remember how. I won't give up. If she's out there, I'll find her. I know she still loves you."

Father Mark paused. He hadn't seen his sister for many years. She was a chronic alcoholic and had been living on the streets, eluding the help he wanted to give her. He sighed. Their mother had clung to the belief that Katherine would eventually return home.

He took a sack of Reese's peanut butter cups out of his bottom drawer. Nothing like chocolate to soothe the troubled soul. He ate a few and realized he'd forgotten to get supper. That was okay. The diner would still be open.

Father Mark loved the warm comfort of the diner's beef stew. He ordered a second serving. As he wiped the bowl with a piece of bread, he remembered he needed to lose weight. He shook off the thought. He wanted dessert, and he was going to have it.

The waitress wore snug jeans, and her top showed healthy shoulders. She smiled as she brought him his pie and refreshed his coffee.

Dear God, Father Mark thought. *I need a wife.*

He gave the perky waitress a tired smile and ordered another piece of pie.

"Hopeless," he muttered as he stood and dropped a few bills on the table.

He needed to do something to cheer himself up. He would listen to the new CDs when he got home. He told himself he wasn't ashamed that he had taken them. It was time he got something for himself. Little enough it was.

His cell phone rang as he turned to leave. It was Connie, and she wasn't happy.

"You took advantage of me," she said. "You shouldn't have done that. I'm a married woman, and you're a priest." She wasn't raising her voice, but Father Mark could hear how upset she was. He was concerned for her, but what was she talking about?

"Connie," he interrupted, trying to be soothing. "What's the matter?"

"You seduced me," she said. "It was your fault."

"Surely you won't deny it was our mutual choice. . . ."

"You made me sin," she insisted.

"Connie," he said, "we've known each other for years. This doesn't have to ruin our friendship."

"Oh, you'll admit it's your fault after I sue you," she said, and hung up.

Father Mark sat back down. His heart was pounding. He wiped the sweat from his face with a stew-stained paper napkin.

"Dear God. Dear God," he said aloud. "How did this happen?"

An Offending Priest

When Father Mark came to see me, he was in his clerical garb, the traditional black robes of a priest. A tall man with a salt-

and-pepper beard, he was significantly overweight. He had an exaggerated enthusiasm that suggested a boy in a man's body. I found myself liking him at once.

"Well, you know, Ken, my good friend," he began, "I've had some trouble. I seem to have had some encounters with women. I know that I'm a bit responsible, but these women invited me. Now I've got one that's angry, and she's threatening to file a lawsuit.

"They say you deal with sexual issues and addictions," he went on. "I guess I might be addicted to food. I *do* eat too much. The doctor's after me. I saw a psychologist some time ago. Nice man. I probably didn't see him enough. I'm still a mess. Too much gluttony and lust. No problem with sloth, though." He laughed.

Father Mark considered Connie a friend. He had seen her often as they worked on church projects together, and she helped him with a soup kitchen he had organized. He felt she had approached him, and he had reciprocated. Now she claimed differently. He was more disturbed by the withdrawal of her friendship than by the prospect of legal trouble. He was hurt, and he didn't understand what had happened.

"I want to do the right thing," he told me. "Should I call her? Should I make amends? I don't think it was really all my fault. But what should I do? I don't want to be sued. I don't want her to feel bad either. She's had a hard life. Her husband is never home. He works two jobs for minimum wage. And she's had six children to raise. She's caring for her mother too. I thought being loving with me was what she wanted. I thought I was comforting her. Why is she so angry? What did I do?"

"What did you do?" I said.

"I don't know," he protested. "She calls me up, she says,

'You seduced me.' It was awful. She said it right out of the blue. It's what's brought me here, that phone call. She was blaming me, saying it was my fault."

"So, those are the questions you want to look at with me?" I asked. "What is your responsibility? What should you do?"

"That's it," he agreed.

"Okay," I said. "You seem anxious about deciding whether you should contact her and talk about this. What if you were to postpone that until you have some better understanding? If she calls, tell her that you will get back to her. Tell her you'll be happy to acknowledge your side of the responsibility. You're just trying to sort this out and get some counseling."

He did tell her that, and he said she accepted his request. So the crisis of the moment passed, but having come to see me, he decided to continue. He was intelligent and self-aware enough to realize he needed help.

⸻

I spent the first sessions finding out about his patterns. He had had other women in his office. They would come to him for counseling, and one thing would lead to another. He insisted they were always adult women. He claimed he was more "the seduced" than "the seducer," but that wasn't clear to me. There seemed to be some loss of boundaries for him. He was some-how exploiting his position of power without quite understand-ing how he did it.

He had been in denial for most of his life about his need for a woman. He felt emotionally deprived. When women were willing, he could not hold himself back. He had had six to ten of these affairs in a twenty-year period. His pattern—as inap-propriate as it was—was not the pattern of a calculating sexual predator. It was more immature, clueless, and compulsive than that, although clearly he was abusing his authority.

There was also the issue of his regular shoplifting. Nobody knew he was doing it until he told me. Even though he felt entitled, it bothered his conscience.

He knew he was crossing boundaries with his behavior, but he was confused about where the boundaries were. When he was telling me about his misdeeds, he did a lot of laughing and joking, which I attributed to his embarrassment, shame, and anxiety.

What became clear to me after only a few sessions was that he was a burned-out caretaker. Like many priests I have treated, he had long suppressed and denied his personal and intimate needs. He was bitter and resentful about having to give up so much. In these early sessions, I was already wondering what he had been required to give up as a child.

"It sounds like you're carrying some resentment," I said to him, "and you're feeling needy and burned out and you're losing your boundaries."

"Oh, yes," he agreed, relieved to be able to say it. "That's exactly right. I don't have good boundaries. How do I take care of that?"

"Let's begin by being very clear about what boundaries you're going to keep."

The first thing was to deal with his offending behavior. He agreed to refer future counseling sessions with women to his associate pastor. If any woman came by unexpectedly, he was to keep his office door open.

"These *are* losses," I consoled him. "Setting boundaries involves choosing to accept certain defined losses."

"That's so hard for me," he said.

"Nobody finds it easy."

Over that first year that he saw me, it turned out that two of the women he had had sexual relations with kept calling him, wanting to come visit him in his office. He had a hard time saying no to them. Their persistence was torture for him, but he held the line mostly. One woman did come to his office unannounced, and "somehow" they ended up on his couch. He told me he remembered his new resolve before it was "too late."

SYMPTOMS OF MEM:
People Pleasing

A MEM will often come into therapy complaining that he is doing too much for others. He learned to placate his mother, and he has carried this way of relating into adulthood, particularly with women. However, it is a difficult False Self to maintain. He commonly gets resentful and acts out his suppressed anger.

Father Mark's dilemma was that he couldn't say no to any request. If someone knocked on his door at midnight, he had to try to help them. The only relief he had was folk music. He had learned to play the guitar as a child, and he was comfortable enough with it to face the open stage Wednesday nights at The Ark in Ann Arbor. In his rare alone time, he listened to his cherished vintage LPs with a collector's delight and a performer's appreciation. The joy of his life was to find the time and money to go to concerts of the folk groups he loved. He had started collecting CDs, and recently he'd gotten some concert DVDs. He was stealing them, because he couldn't afford to buy what he wanted. He got a small priest's pension, and his living quarters were provided, but he had little discretionary income.

As we worked together, he began to clean up his life. He stopped shoplifting. Other than the one slip, he stopped seeing women for sex, although a few continued to call him. Connie had occasional contact with him in connection with activities at the church. She wasn't pressing him, and she didn't follow through on her threat of legal action. But she did remain angry, and he was distressed by that. He made attempts to take responsibility, but she seemed dissatisfied with anything he said. I suggested to him that her response might be a sign that some old anger of hers was being "displaced" onto him. He seemed confused by this, so I suggested one possibility.

"Connie might be angry at her philandering father, for example, who may have betrayed her mother with other women. Connie might be unconsciously displacing that anger onto you, because she now views you as a betrayer of her trust. She may

---

DISPLACED ANGER

When a person is angry with someone from the past, such as a mother or father, he or she may project this anger toward someone in the present. This person in the present usually has some quality that is evocative of the person from the past. Displacement of anger can also happen with respect to circumstances rather than people—for example, the suppressed anger from having to live as a child under abusive conditions might be evoked by some circumstance in the present that is suggestive of those conditions in the past.

have been inhibited from being angry at her father, but she's not inhibited from being angry at you."

The Hollow Helper

Some people naturally can devote themselves to charitable works and at the same time take care of their own emotional and physical needs. They are caretakers with boundaries. However, MEM often become caretakers in a different spirit. They have learned the role of caretaker by being forced to take care of their mothers. They don't know about boundaries. They don't know how to say no. MEM fall into caretaking professions easily, but over time a residue of denied and unreconciled need builds up.

> **FUNDAMENTAL CHARACTERISTICS OF MEM:**
> **The Lost Identity**
>
> A MEM loses contact with himself. He is detached from his own feelings, wants, and needs. He learned at an early age to take care of his mother and to discount himself. This crushing of his emerging self in childhood divorces him from the soul of his individuality. His identity is lost.

These "MEM caretakers" live for others without having a "self" to center them. Their "Lost Identities" leave them vulnerable to be ruled by the Disloyalty Bind. They are eager to placate anybody else's unhappiness, yet they neglect their own needs. Because many of their life choices do not reflect who they are, they are fundamentally unhappy and dissatisfied.

The MEM caretaker "wakes up" in middle life to discover

he has an overwhelming sense of deprivation. He is torn in his unconscious with two unresolved needs: to be cared for and to become himself. He now feels trapped in his caretaker role. He has lost the life he really wanted, the one driven by his own desire, the one energized from his soul rather than his guilt. But often he feels too old to start over again. All his heart's desire seems out of reach. And his despair can be overwhelming,

Given to God

I wanted to learn about Father Mark's family of origin. "How did you become such a caretaker?" I asked him. "Can you tell me about your background?"

His father, Brian, and his mother, Nancy, had grown up in the same neighborhood of Chicago. Brian had felt obligated to marry Nancy when she got pregnant. He went into the army soon after, liked it, and made it his career. But Nancy hated army life. She missed her mother and her friends. She was angry at Brian, who was never home to help her. The baby, Katherine, was born while Brian was in Korea. Nancy was too depressed to show her daughter much joy or give her much attention. Katherine was raised by television and discouraged by neglect.

Before Brian's first tour of Vietnam, he settled his wife and daughter, already twelve, back in the old neighborhood in Chicago. Nancy was delighted. Her spirits rose. Their parting lovemaking unexpectedly yielded baby Mark, born while his father was training the South Vietnamese army. Six years later, to avoid a fourth tour of Vietnam, his father took advantage of the army's policy of allowing retirement after twenty years. Brian was just forty-one. He didn't have any civilian skills, and he felt awkward at home. He idled in his favorite bars, where there was cheerful company. He stayed drunk most of the day.

At first, Nancy tried to make the family function. At suppertime, she sent Mark to tour the bars to bring his father home. But at home, Brian missed his bar buddies, and he resented his overweight, middle-age, depressed wife. Nancy had energy for only a few months of trying.

Katherine was bitter and defiant by the time the family returned to Chicago, but Mark found solace in the neighborhood. He was a gregarious little boy, full of fun and life, and people liked him. He played in the streets with the parish priest, and the priest had taught him how to play the guitar. Although the neighborhood had a certain toughness, Mark felt safe and had a few regular playmates.

Katherine ran away before she finished high school. She sent her mother an occasional postcard from different places, but there was never a return address.

Nancy's emotional state turned even more hopeless when her mother died. Her daughter was gone, and her husband was a drunk. Most people she had known in the neighborhood had moved on. She turned to her son as her last option.

Mark understood that his mother needed help and that his father was not going to provide it. Many times he listened as his mother cried and complained, mostly about his father. Often she would take Mark to her bed and have him sleep next to her. Although there was no genital contact, this bed-sharing went on for years. He provided her with the emotional support she needed to tolerate her alcoholic and neglectful husband, her congenital pessimism, and her depression.

When Mark was in high school, his mother urged him to be a priest. He liked the idea. The prospect of dating was making him very anxious. The Disloyalty Bind was causing him to feel guilty for lusting after all the pretty girls in his classes. His early commitment to become a priest gave him an excuse to stay faithful to his mother and helped him suppress his sexual needs. Only much later would these suppressed needs reemerge.

His childhood had all the elements of mother-son enmeshment: His father had removed himself from the family, not through divorce or death but through work, alcoholism, and emotional withdrawal. His mother had no close adult friends or relatives. She turned to Mark, not as her first choice but as her desperate last choice. And he was eager to help her. As he got older, she realized he might be leaving, and she could not bear the idea of parting with him. In her unconscious, the thought of him ever going to "another woman" was frightening. The priesthood was a compromise. By giving himself to God, he remained faithful to her.

Eating Himself to Death

In his second year of therapy, Father Mark succeeded in maintaining his boundaries around sex and shoplifting, but his compulsive eating had not improved. If anything, it was getting worse.

He was conscientious and wanted to be a good priest, but his unmet needs were draining his life force. He longed for an intimate relationship with a woman. If he could have been a married priest, he would still have had some problems, but the compulsive force behind them would have been much more manageable. As it was, being a priest left him in a state of perpetual neglect, even though he couldn't imagine another life.

In spite of urgings from his doctor, he didn't exercise and his weight wasn't going down. I was worried. I saw that the therapy I was offering was having some significant results, but his ability to marshal his resources in the service of himself was weak.

Mother-enmeshed men have a tendency to neglect themselves. This was becoming Father Mark's key issue and my key concern for him.

SYMPTOMS OF MEM:
Self-Neglect

Many MEM do not feel comfortable taking time or resources for themselves. Even tending to their own necessities can feel "wrong" or "wasteful." A MEM has been trained to focus on only his mother's needs; his needs are expendable. Sometimes even having a little fun can seem dangerous.

Father Mark would promise to diet and exercise, but he didn't do it. In a very real sense, he had given up. I questioned him about this, and he said, "Yeah, maybe somewhat. I don't know. I really don't want to give up." This ambivalence expressed the conflict between his conscious thoughts and his unconscious feelings. As a child, he felt he had to sacrifice himself and take care of others. Food had been his way of compensating for not feeling loved. His unconscious mind carried this despair from his childhood. He was living a life not of reconciliation or acceptance but of resignation. I was worried that he was going to kill himself by ruining his health. But he wasn't consciously suicidal.

Since the demands of the parish were grinding him down, I suggested he take a leave of absence. His doctor agreed with me. Father Mark's high blood pressure and high cholesterol were not responding to treatment, and his weight was going up instead of down. He resisted. He said too many people de-

pended on him. He insisted he couldn't be "slothful." But finally, exhausted, he gave in and agreed to take a leave from his
duties as priest and to allow others to run the food bank.

Father Mark Chooses Life

He was relieved of all his duties. For the first time since he was
five, the only person he had to take care of was himself.

It was during this leave that the Chicago police called him.
A homeless woman had been discovered dead by city sanitation
workers. She had claimed to her buddies that she had a brother
who was a priest in Detroit. Could this be him? Father Mark
went to Chicago to identify his sister, Katherine. He brought
her back to Detroit, and the parish arranged a burial for her.
Then something unusual happened. The time for his leave
ended, but Father Mark decided he wasn't ready to go back to
work. He also took some time off from therapy.

A few months later, he called and said he wanted to start up
with me again. He was no longer in his clerical garb; he was
dressed like a workman in plaid shirt and khaki workpants. He
had shaved his beard and lost weight. But also, his manner had
undergone a subtle but significant shift. He was no longer the
jolly caretaker. He was more serious, almost with an edge of
anger, certainly with a new firmness. I could see his father, the
professional soldier, in him.

"I'm so sorry about your sister," I said.

"So many years," he began, and thereafter our sessions considered the many faces of loss.

❦

Father Mark had begun going to Overeaters Anonymous meet-
ings and became a passionate devotee and advocate of the OA

program. He walked to the library for exercise, checking out all the folk music he could find and reading books on its origins and history. He continued to write his deceased mother and sister letters as a part of his process to ease his grief. Some of our sessions were just him reading the letters to me.

When we decided he could stop regular therapy eight months later, he had maintained his weight loss of almost fifty pounds. He had extended his leave with the parish. He was thinking about resigning from the priesthood and continuing his charitable work as a social worker. He was also thinking about getting married. These were complicated decisions, but I was confident that he was ready to face them.

"My understanding was weak," he said to me on parting, "but I wanted to do the right thing. That was sufficient for God to show mercy. I'm sad about the loss of time," he admitted, "but I'm with myself at last."

I took that to mean he was at peace.

Suicidal Self-Sacrifice

The MEM caretaker fools himself into believing he has chosen a life of sacrifice rather than having it imposed upon him. Mother-son enmeshment is an inversion of the parent-child relationship. Instead of the mother being attuned to the needs of the child, the mother has insisted that the child be attuned to hers. (See Figure 4-1.) As an adult, the MEM caretaker acts out this inversion by being attuned to everybody but himself. Eventually, this living in his False Self burns him out.

The inversion of the parent-child relationship, along with the child's need to move away from his mother, causes the stress that creates the Disloyalty Bind and the Lost Identity, the two fundamental consequences of enmeshment. The MEM does

Mother Attuned to Son: He Can Be Himself

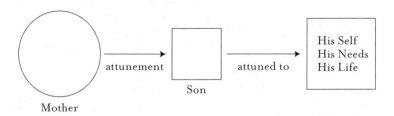

Son Attuned to Mother: He Loses His Identity

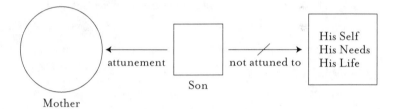

Figure 4-1. When a mother is attuned to her son, he can have his own life. When a son must be attuned to his mother, his outward energy is blocked. He is trapped with her and must devote his life to serving her needs. In adulthood, the MEM remains attuned to the needs of others at the expense of his own.

not develop his individual identity. In the language of developmental psychology, he has not successfully completed his "individuation."

The enmeshed little boy feels considerable anger, but the anger has to be suppressed in the service of staying attached to his mother. However, the anger does not go away and often is later projected onto other people. If it is also projected onto himself (as in the case of Father Mark), the MEM can become a living mechanism of self-destruction.

The burned-out caretaker wants to stop being always on

call, because he is exhausted. He can't consciously choose to stop, but his unconscious is operating at a more primitive level. It prefers a stopped wreck to a continuation of the journey. Eventually, the unconscious mind has its way, in spite of the conscious will. The unconscious tells the body, "I'm tired. I've had enough," and then it pulls the emergency stop: heart attack, stroke, aneurysm. . . .

Some organizations and societies encourage individuals to live lives of suicidal self-sacrifice. But people who are drawn to live this way often cause themselves emotional and spiritual damage. This damage inevitably gets passed on to the next generation, which in turn passes it on to the next, and so on. The resulting chain of grief is ultimately less beneficial to society than allowing people to experience their true desires and make their own true emotional connections. People who are free to desire without guilt can follow their love and pursue their dreams. They bequeath to future generations fertile ground for the development of healthy children and mature adults.

Father Mark found his way past self-destruction. His path was still challenging, but the challenges were life enhancing rather than life destroying.

✑

Not all people-pleasing MEM caretakers are humble parish priests. There is a more grandiose version, as exemplified by Warren, the politician, as we shall see in Chapter 6.

In the next chapter, we learn about Sam. In spite of being newly married to a wonderful woman, he got caught up in sex on the Internet and began to prefer his computer to his wife. Cybersex is the crack cocaine of pornography and can become a serious addiction. MEM are particularly vulnerable to it. Breaking free requires the same types of interventions needed to get past a drug addiction: psychotherapy, twelve-step support groups, and (in cases where a relationship is being damaged) couples counseling.

5 SAM LOVES HIS COMPUTER
The Cybersex Addict

Carol lay in bed alone waiting for Sam. He had said he'd be right up, but that was more than an hour ago. This was still their honeymoon year. Shouldn't he be eager to come to her? But she knew what he was doing, and finally she got up and went downstairs.

Sam was at his computer. He didn't notice her as she walked up behind him. A woman posed on screen. Carol touched Sam on the shoulder.

"Oh, hi, honey," he said, turning off the monitor. "I didn't hear you. I'm coming right up."

"It's been an hour."

"Really? I thought it was just a couple of minutes."

She reached over and turned the monitor back on. "You like this stuff?"

He used the mouse to close the browser. "Not exactly," he said. "There's a lot of it out there. It's hard to avoid."

"You've got a real woman here," she said, sitting on his lap. She put her arms around his neck and kissed him. "Remember?"

"I'm sorry, honey."

She kissed him again. "Aren't I better than anything on that computer?"

"No contest," he agreed.

Upstairs, however, he was distracted. He went though the motions without looking at her.

"Where are you?" she asked, but he didn't answer.

> **SYMPTOMS OF MEM:**
> **Sexual Problems**
>
> A MEM's sexuality is wounded by enmeshment. The effects in adulthood can include sexual dysfunction, sexual anorexia (avoidance of sex), sexual addiction, and sexual perversions. A MEM's wounded sexuality is also a significant component of the low self-worth and the chronic depression, ambivalence, and rage that plague many MEM.

Carol Fights Back

Carol told me she had been a model, but she now owned a small advertising agency. She spent some time telling me what a wonderful man Sam was. They had met when they both stopped to help a dog that had been hit in traffic and abandoned. They liked each other, intimacy came as an easy consequence of friendship, and marriage followed.

His change six months into their marriage had blindsided her.

"He was always so loving and attentive. Now it's like he's avoiding me. Even when we make love, he's distant. It's like he's not there, or *I'm* not there. It feels lonely."

"Has there been any change that you can think of? Some

conflict between you? Or maybe something has changed for him at work?"

"Not really. We've known each other for almost three years. We work hard, with two businesses, but we always had time to be loving before. I don't think anything really changed. Well, he does get upset about his mother."

"He does?"

"He calls her every Friday, and he hates it. He hates to call her, but he always does it anyway. Sam doesn't complain, but I can tell talking to her upsets him. He always has a couple of beers the minute he hangs up. She's a pretty negative person. I'm afraid she doesn't like me very much either."

"She doesn't like you?"

"Sometimes people take one look at me and decide they're not going to like me," she acknowledged. "It was that way with her. Sam brought me to see her, and she just glowered. She didn't give me a chance to show her how much I love her son and would like to love her. I don't know what people see that makes them hate me. I'm really very nice."

"You told me on the phone that he didn't want to come with you to see me, that he didn't think there was a problem. Did you let him know how concerned you are?"

"Yes, but he doesn't see any change in our connection. At least that's what he says."

I waited.

"There is one thing," she offered after a while. "He's been on the computer a lot, and so he doesn't come to bed until late."

"What's he doing?"

"I guess it's some kind of porn. He changes channels when I show up, but I've seen some pretty sexy pictures."

"What do you think about that?"

"I don't like it."

"How much time does he spend on the computer?"

"Too much, Hours."

"Every day?"

"Every night. Until late. He avoids me to be on the computer. And when we make love, he's not there with me anymore. That's what really bothers me. He's not with me, even when he's with me. He says I'm imagining it, but I'm not. He's says it's the same as always, but I know it isn't."

"He denies he's doing it?"

"He says I'm making a big deal of nothing. But it isn't so!"

"You're concerned that he's drifted away from you," I said, and she nodded yes. "You see him spending more and more time on the computer, looking at sexy pictures, and he's not as *there* for you as before. Especially, he seems to be preoccupied even when you're making love."

"Yes," she said.

"I think there is a problem here," I said. "You aren't making a big deal of nothing. Sometimes I see a progression in the use of pornography on the Internet. Occasional use can become regular use, and this can lead to a full-fledged addiction. The withdrawal from you into cybersex is something other clients of mine have reported. I've known cybersex addicts who spent hundreds of dollars at a sitting on pay sites, neglected their relationships, logged in at work and got fired, and ended up getting divorced.

"The best way to make progress," I told her, "would be to have him come here too. Do you think he would do that, now that I've agreed with you that there may be a problem?"

"I'll try," Carol promised.

Sexual Addiction

Healthy people use their sexual energy to initiate contact and to bond. A romantic bond is an expression of interest in another person. It is an expression of desire. That can be a problem for a MEM. He may have difficulty expressing his sexuality with a woman he's interested in, because he's too conflicted in his feelings for his mother. But he's got to do something with his sexual energy, so he takes it out of the arena of romance and bonding and into fantasy and masturbation. Over time, this kind of solitary sexual expression can become addictive, because it's detached from the other parts of his life and from his value system. This addictive process is described in *Out of the Shadows: Understanding Sexual Addiction* by Patrick Carnes.

Cybersex

What's the big deal about cybersex? Hasn't pornography always been available? Cybersex is much more addictive than other forms of pornography. On the Internet, an addict can quickly find exactly what he wants. Further, there are no social barriers, such as the possible shame associated with going out and buying pornography, and there are no physical barriers, such as having to drive out in a snowstorm to find an open drugstore at midnight or being seen going into clubs or brothels by neighbors or colleagues. The MEM cybersex addict feels powerful in his anonymity, control, and choice, in contrast to the powerlessness and inadequacy he felt when he was being enmeshed by his mother.

I am aware of many case histories of people with no previous problems with pornography becoming addicted to cybersex. My own caseload of cybersex addicts has increased dramatically over the last ten years.

CHECKLIST FOR CYBERSEX ADDICTION

This checklist has been adapted from Patrick Carnes et al., In
the Shadows of the Net: Breaking Free of Compulsive Online
Sexual Behavior *(Center City, MN: Hazelden, 2001), pp. 22–26.*

❑ *Being preoccupied with sex on the Internet*

❑ *Engaging in cybersex more often or for longer periods of
time than intended*

❑ *Attempting unsuccessfully to control, reduce, or stop using
cybersex*

❑ *Becoming restless or irritable following any attempt to
control, reduce, or stop using cybersex*

❑ *Using cybersex as an escape from problems or to relieve
feelings, such as helplessness, guilt, anxiety, or depression*

❑ *Searching continually for a more intense or higher-risk
cybersex experience*

❑ *Lying to conceal involvement with cybersex*

❑ *Engaging in illegal cybersex (e.g., child pornography or
soliciting)*

❑ *Jeopardizing or losing a significant relationship or job
because of cybersex*

❑ *Incurring significant financial consequences as a result of
cybersex*

ॐ

Love in Spite of Porn

Sam and Carol came to see me together a few weeks after I had
met with Carol. In the waiting room, they were holding hands:
Carol supportive, Sam nervous. This waiting-room behavior
was significant and not at all typical. Most often, when a couple

comes to see me about pornography, they are in a crisis of angry confrontation.

I met with them on a regular basis for several months, and the core of their situation emerged fairly quickly. Sam had a crippling enmeshed relationship with his mother, and he used cybersex to soothe his fear of engulfment and feelings of inadequacy and to discharge his anger. Carol's difficulty was with her husband's isolating himself from her. However, there were other factors, including the pressures of Sam's work and his use of alcohol.

To help give a fuller sense of what Sam and Carol were dealing with, I've developed the following reconstruction of "Sam's week." It illustrates how the lives of addicted MEM are driven and controlled by their enmeshment issues.

Sam's Week: Feel Bad, Avoid Carol, Drink, Do Porn, Masturbate

Sam's week began with his Friday night phone call to his mother. He dreaded the call, which he dutifully made every week. No matter what they talked about, he hung up reinforced in his sense that he was never quite doing enough for her, that he didn't measure up to expectations, that he was a disappointment, and that he was inadequate no matter how hard he tried.

The phone call alone wasn't going to make him feel this way. A normally functioning man, who talks occasionally with his mother on the phone and feels a little guilty when she reminds him that they haven't talked for a while, isn't going to be deeply affected or affected for a long time. He will feel a moment of guilt, promise her and himself that he will do better in the future, and then let it go. The effect on Sam was profoundly different. The call was a "booster shot" to his childhood inoculation of enmeshment. He felt an "emotional hangover" all week that clouded his relationship with Carol, dampened his enthusiasm at work, and in the evenings, when the bad feelings were especially intense, drove his cybersex addiction.

He avoided Carol because (projecting from his relationship with his mother) he didn't want to be further intruded on or made to feel guilty again. He especially did not want to feel inadequate, which was the way his mother always made him feel.

At work, he was also feeling inadequate. He didn't trust his judgment, and he asked employees who knew less than he did for help and advice. He kept making apologies to his partner, who couldn't figure out what he was apologizing for. Sam was the chief engineer, as well as co-owner, and he was known as the man to go to for technical problems nobody else could solve. He had been "Mr. Fix-it" for his mother all though his childhood and beyond. Now he was Mr. Fix-it at work. He did it well, but he never felt good about it. He tried extra hard and worked extra-long hours, but he didn't feel that he was doing enough. He got frustrated and found himself becoming suddenly enraged when something went wrong. He yelled and blamed, and then people were afraid of him, and resentful. His bad feelings at work resulted from carrying the heavy load of guilt that his mother had laid on him. Yet he had no conscious awareness that what was happening to him at work had anything to do with his Friday phone call or his childhood.

He left work late, stressed out and brooding about how badly things had gone. The business was making money, but he felt that he was doing an inadequate job. When he got home, Carol wanted to talk and spend time with him. Sometimes she suggested they go out to dinner, because they both worked long hours, and she thought they could relax and have fun. No matter what she wanted, he felt it as pressure. And suddenly he would be angry with her, and she wouldn't understand why he was so angry. What had she done to deserve this? He couldn't tell her. He didn't understand himself.

What's the matter with me? he thought, after Carol—confused and hurt—had left him alone. *To hell with it. I need a break.* So he had a drink and watched TV. And had another drink. TV was boring, so he turned on the computer and went online. He found his favorite sites. This was more like it. These women didn't pressure him. They didn't make him feel inadequate. Quite the opposite. He felt free. He felt competent and powerful, and he got erect, whereas with Carol lately that had been a problem. But with these cyber-women he could enjoy sex, and nobody was making him feel guilty.

This was the way his week went. Every day he felt bad at work, he avoided Carol, he had a few drinks at night, and then he found soothing relief with his cybersex babes. Then he felt bad again.

On Friday he dutifully called his mother.

The Sexual Development of MEM

Sexuality doesn't begin in adolescence. It begins long before that and is strongly imprinted by experiences in childhood, particularly by relationships with primary caretakers. The love between a mother and father naturally disrupts enmeshment. *I love my mommy. She's very pretty, but she's Daddy's.* That's the way it's supposed to be. (See Figure 5-1.)

But usually in the case of a MEM, his father is distant and his mother is too close. So the mother-enmeshed little boy is exposed to sexual feelings that are more than he can deal with. (See Figure 5-2.)

Healthy Adult Intimacy Boundary

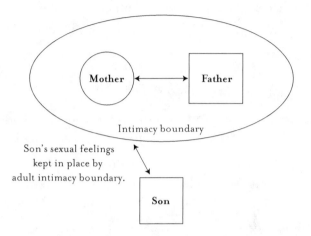

Figure 5-1. Mother and Father together protect the son from enmeshment by maintaining an intimate connection. When the little boy says, "Mommy, I want to marry you," the mother responds, "That's so sweet, honey. But I'm already married to Daddy."

A child's sexual awareness is not supposed to be so intense so early. It's not supposed to feel so overtly erotic. It is supposed to be free and innocent, and guided by the child's own develop-

Unhealthy Adult Intimacy Boundary

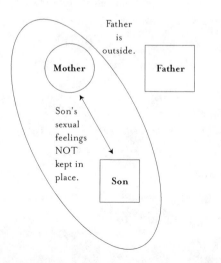

Figure 5-2. With father "outside," the natural barrier to enmeshment is gone. When the little boy says, "Mommy, I want to marry you," she might respond, "I'm so lonely. That father of yours is never home. You can keep mommy company."

mental process, not the mother's neediness. But if she is emotionally dependent on her son, rather than the other way around, there is no healthy containment of the child's developing sexuality.

The Sexual Wound of MEM

There are two components to a MEM's sexual wound. First, as explained above, a MEM's sexuality is aroused too early, and it is not moderated by a healthy mother-father bond. Second, a little boy cannot be made to feel exploited, intruded on, and trapped by his mother without his budding masculinity and sexuality absorbing the force of the blow. These two factors create a sexual wound that goes deep and straight to the center of his being. It is not healed by the passage of time. In adulthood, it leads to a gap between love and lust, which in turn can drive the various sexual and emotional problems of MEM that we've noted here and in earlier chapters.

The Gap Between Love and Lust

A mother-enmeshed child's early sexual feelings can be so overaroused and infiltrated by the pain of enmeshment that he has to "contain them" by putting them in a sealed-off, special compartment in his mind. Thereafter, he does not naturally relate sexual feelings and loving feelings to each other. As an adult, he may be very loving toward his wife while expressing his sexuality separate from her. John Money, in his classic clinical text, *Lovemaps,* points out that sexual perversions—which are often played out in isolation of values and commitments—are the result of the gap between love and lust.

The most fundamental cause of these various sexual problems for MEM is that the primary bond with the mother in the early years of life has been corrupted. The various elements noted above are "details," but the "disruption of early attachment," in clinical language, is the basis of all the trouble. This dynamic is discussed further in Chapter 14, which is about parenting.

Repairing the Damage

Although Sam and Carol both had focused on his sexual issues, Sam's need to have multiple drinks every night suggested to me a possible additional problem with compulsive alcohol use. Some of the danger signs of alcohol dependency in his behavior include his regular use, the lack of a social element to his drinking, his tendency to drink to escape painful feelings, and the "need" to have a drink.

I recommended individual therapy for Sam to help him learn to stop using cybersex and alcohol and to help him understand why he felt the need to escape from his beautiful loving wife. He agreed to work with me, and I suggested a marriage counselor, so they could continue their couples work. It would be good for them to have a monthly check-in with a counselor, until Sam was ready for more.

It took Sam about six months to have his first aha! moment. He had been realizing how much anger at women he had and how much he feared them. Then it hit him: "It's not *women*. It's *my mother*. I get really upset when I'm talking to my mother." He felt the thrill of this discovery. "I feel guilty and get angry, and I need to have a few drinks and go online. I get upset just thinking about her."

During the same six months, Sam had gone through my basic addiction program. He was making good progress in managing his addictions. His resulting new clarity contributed to his ability to understand the issues from his childhood—in particular, with his mother—that drove his need for cybersex and alcohol. Sam also became aware of the phenomenon of "triggering." Something that happened in the present could remind his unconscious mind of something that had happened in the past. Then his unconscious would release a flood of old feelings that he would confuse with feelings about the present. And he would want to drink and go on the Internet.

After Sam had stopped using sex and alcohol compulsively, he and Carol began to see their marriage counselor once a week. Now, with Sam becoming sober, they were in a position to work on their communication skills and especially on rebuilding their intimacy. Now when Carol felt Sam "slipping away from her" during sex or at other times, she could talk with him about it. At the same time, when Sam was having a difficult time, when he was craving relief by using sexual fantasies and cybersex, he could let his wife know what was going on without fearing ridicule or dismissive anger.

By the end of his first year of treatment, Sam hadn't used cybersex for many months. He understood that he was a MEM, and he realized what this meant about his behavior patterns. He saw that his contacts with his mother needed to have more boundaries.

He let his mother know that he was not always available for her. He broke the pattern of the weekly call. I helped him prepare for her reaction and his own fear of retaliation and his guilt. He tried to make this change with his mother more positive by helping her develop other outlets and connections. (Chapter 11 discusses these types of strategies in detail.)

As Sam made progress in therapy, he needed to do something to help him claim his masculine presence and identity in the face of his MEM experiences. In other words, he had to learn to identify with men. In a healthy childhood, this task would have been achieved through contact with his father. Sam found it helpful to join a men's therapy group, where other men were dealing with similar issues.

Then one day Sam sat down and said to me, "I get it now. My cybersex wasn't just a fun way to relax and get turned on. I was avoiding something. I was managing anxiety and saying 'to hell with you' to Mom. I was trying to convince myself that she didn't control me." All at once, the whole story came into focus for him.

Sex, Romance, and Desire

We can gain significant insight into the sexual difficulties of MEM by considering the question: What's the difference between a mother-enmeshed woman and a MEM? A mother-enmeshed woman has an emotional template similar to a MEM. As with a MEM, a mother-enmeshed woman is going to be a caretaker. Her major way of relating to others is "How can I help you?" A mother-enmeshed woman may be drawn to get involved romantically with a MEM. Her denial of her own enmeshment causes her to be unable to see his, and an enmeshed relationship seems natural to her because of her childhood experiences.

But in the damage to his sexuality, there is a significant difference between a mother-enmeshed woman and a MEM. A daughter has to be separate from her mother, but she doesn't have to be fundamentally different from her mother. A boy has to be separate and different from his mother in a way that allows him to become the man he is destined to be. In mother-son enmeshment, there is a sexual boundary that is violated by the enmeshment. It functions in the MEM's spirit as emotional incest, also referred to as psychological incest or covert incest. My first book, *Silently Seduced,* uses "covert incest," while *The Emotional Incest Syndrome* by Patricia Love and Jo Robinson uses the term in the title. Both of these books are about parent-child enmeshment.

Psychologist Eugene Monick puts it this way in his book *Castration and Male Rage:* "The result of psychological incest is the son's using the mother as model rather than the father, seeing the world through her eyes, sensing the world through her senses. Since she is feminine, such an identification is injurious to his discovery of himself as masculine."

The bond with the mother for a MEM is stronger, more romantic, and more tinged with sexual energy than for a mother-enmeshed woman. As a result, a MEM tends to have more conflict regarding his normal desire for sex, romance, intimacy, and commitment. Typically, the mother-enmeshed woman is less sexually encumbered, while the MEM is heavily burdened with fundamental doubt and shame regarding his erotic impulses. The ability to have a successful romantic relationship requires, among other things, an unencumbered ability for sexual desire. Thus, a number of MEM are sexual anorexics; in other words, they fear and suppress their sexuality. This is discussed in the book *Sexual Anorexia* by Patrick Carnes with Joseph Moriarity.

Even when a MEM is sexually active, he may be compulsively acting out his anxiety and guilt and his inability to use his sexual energy to bond. His sexuality is so burdened that it cannot function normally to help him be emotionally present for sexual intimacy. Instead, his sexual energy is dissipated in masturbation and masturbation-like sexual intercourse. There he avoids the "danger" of commitment and "frees himself" from his mother's hold on his sexual energy. Although womanizing and other forms of nonintimate, noncommitted sexual acting out might seem less isolating, they are not. They may be just as detached as masturbation.

Sam Prefers His Wife to Porn

At the end of three years of treatment, Sam and Carol had created a new life together and no longer needed therapy. Sam has boundaries in place with his mother that both of them understand. He limits his helping her to things that feel okay for him. He also won't let her badmouth Carol. He helps his mother do things that develop her independence, like going to the community center. He doesn't necessarily agree to do things for her that keep her dependent on him, such as running errands, doing chores, and giving her money on a routine basis. (See Chapter 11.)

Now Sam prefers his wife to cybersex. Although Internet porn can draw him at times, he remembers the isolated painful feelings that go with it, and that's enough to deter him. It hasn't been an easy journey, but it has been successful. Now he can have his own true woman, and Carol has recovered her loving man.

The Illusion of Freedom

To a MEM, cybersex can seem to be the perfect drug to lift his spirits. When he is online, the women don't make demands on him or try to make him feel guilty. His demoralization is momentarily lifted. Fooled by the illusion of freedom, he thinks, *I'm competent. I'm potent. See, I can function.* Then he collapses, glory forgotten, demoralized again.

Sam responded to therapy, and he turned his life around with the help of Carol. The foundation of his pathway to freedom was Carol's refusal to accept a crippled relationship with her husband. He was only beginning his cybersex addiction, and he responded to standard addiction interventions. Therapy completed his recovery, giving him tools to diminish the pain of his enmeshment and lifting his need for addictive escapes.

❦

Sam was a typical placating MEM, too eager to please, feeling guilty when he wasn't guilty, and soothing his distress through an addictive escape. But there is another kind of MEM, arrogant and feeling entitled, covering his vulnerability by a show of hypermasculinity. My most prominent client was in this second category. He was a powerful politician, whom I call Warren in the next chapter.

6 WHY WARREN WILL NEVER BE PRESIDENT

The Disappointed Hero

Warren watched as the lights from the monuments across the bridge made shimmers in the water. The city was sparkling with an uncommon coating of fresh snow, making the brightly lighted landscape even more brilliant. Warren wondered why he wasn't president. He remembered the golden days of his high potential: star student in high school, full scholarship to George Washington University, Fulbright fellowship to study international law in Geneva. A notable beginning when he entered politics. A poor preacher's son made good, his life had been written up as an inspirational story for a national magazine.

Now all that promise seemed to have drifted away. He had spent his life making friends, and at this moment he had hardly one friend left in town. His potential, his ideals—so real when he was twenty-five, still possible when he was thirty-five—now seemed out of reach. He wondered: *Did I make any worthwhile contribution at all?*

He was a stranger to his family. He had let his children grow up without him. He hadn't seen his wife, Judy, for almost a month. He could call her now, he realized, to tell her he missed her. She would be surprised to hear from him. She might be offended, it had been so long. He decided he didn't want to deal with her reaction.

His aide was waiting for him in the Escalade. There was work to do. It wasn't that late. Plenty of time to answer a few more letters.

He's Never Home, but How Can I Blame Him?

Judy came to see me because she was depressed.

"The doctor insisted I see a psychologist before he would give me something for it," she said. "I'm sorry to bother you. I really don't have anything I want to ask you."

"What do you think you're depressed about?" I asked.

"Oh, nothing. Everything," she said. "I can't say really. I miss Warren. He's so busy, but how can I complain? He's been a public servant for a very long time. He works so hard."

A single tear fell down on the front of her red wool suit. I handed her a Kleenex. She thanked me, daubed at her eyes, and sat looking down.

"I can see you miss him," I said. "Have you talked with him about it?"

She looked up. "Oh, no. I would never do such a thing. The poor man is so burdened as it is. He helps everybody. He is so wonderful to everybody."

"But you miss him?" She nodded. "And you haven't talked with him about your feelings?" She nodded again.

"Do you think he would come with you to see me?" I asked.

To My Surprise, They Agree

Warren was a big man, at least six-three, a bit heavy, but it looked good on him. He smiled when he saw me, shook hands warmly, called me "Kenneth," and asked me how I was. While Warren was greeting me, Judy sat without drawing attention to herself. She gave me a nervous smile but didn't say anything. They sat on separate chairs rather than the couch. Seeing how anxious she was, I asked her permission to summarize what she had told me. That done, I asked Warren for his perspective.

"It's all true, of course," he said, "completely true." His tone conveyed sadness, guilt, and ironic humor. "I have terribly neglected my wonderful wife. We used to be inseparable. Now we hardly see each other. I do miss being with you, honey."

"And I miss you," Judy said. "I know how much work you have to do, but sometimes I really do think that you're avoiding me, keeping me away from you on purpose." She began to cry quietly.

I was impressed by her boldness. She must have been holding this speech in reserve for years. Warren stared at her. I imagined that Judy usually played a passive role.

"Honey," he said, "of course I'm not staying away on purpose. You don't have to cry," he added, but I stopped him.

"Let her cry if she needs to," I said. "What about your feelings?"

"I feel awful," he admitted, and for the first time, it seemed a straight statement. "I do miss Judy. My God, we've been going together since high school, and now we hardly see each other. You know, she was the prettiest cheerleader—"

"Warren," I interrupted. "Your wife is upset about how separate you two have become. I wonder if you have any feelings about that."

"Okay, you're right," he said. "I'll try to be home more. . . ."

"Tell me about your schedule," I asked him. "How did you come to be such a dedicated worker?"

"I've always worked hard, ever since I was a kid. Dad died. I had to take care of Mom." And suddenly he was crying, too, not the quiet tears of his wife, but big messy sobs. I handed him his own Kleenex box and waited.

"It's always been up to me to make things right," he said, after they both calmed down. "Who else was going to do it? I guess I just carried that over into my public life."

Judy gave a sad smile. "I always loved the do-gooder side of you," she said, dabbing absently at her eyes. "It was so sweet. You were such an earnest young man."

They smiled at each other, and I saw the possibility of a renewed connection.

I recommended individual therapy for both of them and was shocked when they both agreed. Warren would work with me, and I recommended a colleague for Judy.

A Golden Childhood

I asked Warren to tell me about the dissatisfactions and stressors associated with his work. He didn't hold back. He was tired of having to take care of everybody. He was exhausted. His doctor had warned him about high blood pressure and had ordered him to lose weight.

He was eager to come clean. His life of many layers had become a burden to him. He felt a loss and disappointment around his career in politics. He had lost his last election, and he didn't have much hopes of a comeback. He sensed something in himself had blunted his potential. When he paused to feel it, he was very sad.

"I've always had to make *other* people happy," he said, "since I was a kid. It was never about what I wanted."

"Tell me about that," I suggested. "Tell me about your childhood."

"Not much to tell, pretty normal childhood. No sisters, one brother, a few years younger than me. My father was a preacher, a gentle man, spent a lot of time writing and practicing his sermons. He was a sweet daddy, never laid a hand on us, died when I was eight, though. That was a difficult time. Mom was devastated. I had to pull us together. And I did too."

"That's impressive," I said. "Can you give me a few more details?"

Warren's father died when his car was smashed by a pickup truck full of drunks. His mother became depressed and withdrawn. Warren took over the running of the household. He heated the TV dinners. He washed the clothes. He put his little brother to bed and helped him get ready for school in the morning. The neighbors looked in from time to time, but the children didn't seem in desperate need.

✑

One day Warren came home from school bursting with pride and enthusiasm. Ignoring his mother's depressed spirits, he said, "I'm going to be in the school play. I'm the only third grader. I get to wear a costume and sing a song. Isn't it great?"

She looked down at him and seemed to bring him into focus from far away. She smiled. "That's wonderful, Warren," she agreed. "Just think, my son, the only third grader."

"Right," he said, beaming with conquest. "I got elected. It was easy. One day I'm going to be president."

"That's wonderful," she said. She was overwhelmed with the idea of it. "My son, the president."

The next day, she emerged from her withdrawal. She talked

to him. She shared her loneliness, her frustration, and her disappointment. She talked about God. She talked about the nobility of suffering. Warren listened, confused but honored. He wanted to please. He wanted to soothe her. She told him how important he was to her, and he felt proud and special. She began to dote on him. He was her shining light, her hero. He was golden.

He kept her company when he wasn't in school, read her the Bible every evening, and kissed her "good night" every night. He continued to help around the house. He no longer played with his friends or his little brother.

At school, Warren also wanted to please, and succeeded. He was liked by his teachers and his classmates. Naturally gregarious and intelligent, he appeared confident and a natural leader. He was not naturally a workaholic but became one. Every achievement he could manage seemed to brighten his mother a little more. She asked him every day about what he had done. She started attending church again and returned to her volunteer work. She loved to brag about him. She became the mirror of his success, and he made himself shine to keep her shining.

One day he found his dead father's secret stash of detective paperbacks. The provocative covers fascinated him, and some of the stories featured sexy dominating women. He started masturbating to these stories. He found for the first time relief from his childhood burden of having to "win the day" for his mother. He could escape from having to manage his mother's grief into a world of pleasure, where a woman would relieve him of having to be the one in control, the "hero." Over time, the occasional relief became a daily compulsion, a secret shameful other life he felt he had to keep hidden from everyone.

On the outside, Warren continued to shine, as he managed

his mother's grief and his shameful secret. In high school, Warren took Judy to the drive-in, and she taught him how to neck. When she began to assume they were engaged, he decided it must be so. Their senior year he was valedictorian, but his pleasure of achievement was muted by exhaustion. He was tired of having to manage his mother's happiness. He was eager to get away.

He and Judy arranged to go to the same college, George Washington University in Washington, D.C. As expected, Warren was outstandingly successful. He even succeeded at appearing to be happy, friendly, helpful, and popular. Warren and Judy married soon after they graduated. He began at once to be a rising political star, with Judy his most loyal ally and supporter. Now that he was married, he hoped his secret sexual life of masturbation to fantasies of dominating women would finally go away.

The Hero People Pleaser

The hero people pleaser is similar to the humble helper (Father Mark from Chapter 4), but he is more grandiose. He is "the man who gets things done." Typically, he is his mother's golden boy rather than her charmer (Doug from Chapter 2) or her mere companion (Sonny from Chapter 1). She lives her life through him. He is her pride, her joy, her trophy. Her life is about reflecting his glory. Although to other people she appears a positive force in his life, because she is his champion and supporter, the truth is that her focus on him is damaging. He feels compelled to live to make his mother proud. What he wants and who he is becomes lost as he focuses on making her happy. In popular culture, boys like Warren are often portrayed as heroes and saviors, while the damage done to them by these inverted parent-child relationships is ignored.

As an adult, the hero MEM still works to impress his mother. Both his guilt and his (usually well-hidden) low self-worth drive his workaholism. He can never do enough for Mom. Even if he is successful, and he often is, there is this nagging feeling that he should have accomplished so much more.

When Warren first came to see me, he exemplified the hero people pleaser. In particular, he was the man with the Lost Identity. There was no Warren. He was whatever you wanted him to be. His political decisions were ruled by the results of polls, but long before polling Warren had been eager to please. He had lived his life to serve others: his mother, his teachers, his constituents. And like other MEM people pleasers, he couldn't say no, even when he needed a break.

Warren was depressed and overwhelmed by the emptiness that he had always felt but had never been able to admit. All his life, he had pretended to be positive and confident, but eventually his despair shut down his ability to live the life dictated by his False Self. First he lost his edge. Then he stopped being successful. Finally he collapsed into an existential crisis. He was suddenly facing his True Self and could no longer maintain the pretense that everything was under control.

Cracking Warren's Code

"What do you do with all this tension?" I asked him one day. "Many men in your position relax with a drink."

"No," he assured me. "I've never touch the stuff. I honor my daddy's memory by avoiding alcohol entirely and urging others to do the same."

"That's fine," I said. "Admirable. Believe me, I've had a lot of clients who should do the same. But still, I've never seen a case like this where the client doesn't have an outlet to relieve his stress." I paused, but he said nothing. "Sex is a common outlet."

"I'm afraid my wife and I have gotten out of the habit. . . ."

"Perhaps sex with someone else?"

"I've never gone with any other woman."

"You might use prostitutes just to let off steam."

"I've never used prostitutes."

"Men?"

"No, not men. Of course not!" He took a breath and studied me. He saw that I was not going to let it go. He sighed. "I do my own 'stress reduction,' " he reluctantly admitted. "Safe, clean, and not likely to get me impeached. Is that a problem?"

"It's not a problem for me," I assured him. "But I'm trying to help you, and it would be useful to know about your sexual practices and fantasies. They always encode a client's core issues. They're a source of insight for therapy."

"Fine," he said, irritated. "You can have all the details you want. Every morning before I get up, I lie there and 'relieve the tension.' It works quite nicely too."

"What do you fantasize about? Is there a common theme?"

"I just imagine a pretty naked lady and masturbate," he said. "Is that so complicated?"

"There's nothing complicated about that," I agreed, "but given your history, I would expect something with a little more drama in it."

"There is a fantasy I like," he admitted. "I read it in an old dime novel a long time ago. It's a story about being dominated by a woman. . . ." He went on to tell me the story. "What do you think of that?" he said, trying to sound humorously ironic.

"I appreciate the fact that you've trusted me enough to tell me your fantasy," I said. "I think we can use it to help you make progress." He looked a little perplexed.

"A fantasy of domination by a woman is common for men who had to be golden boys for their mothers," I said. "Especially men who have high-pressure jobs. They escape the pressure by becoming passive in their fantasies, with somebody else in control."

"So, I masturbate," Warren said. "What's the big deal about that?"

"The problem is, you never get a chance to be who you are. Maybe you have always felt burdened by being your mother's golden boy. Maybe you never did want to be president. How can you tell? You're too numbed to know. And besides, your masturbation is keeping you from your wife. You guys haven't had sex for years. She's upset. She's depressed. Your fantasies don't allow you to connect with her or be true to yourself. My guess is, you've never done what you wanted to do, and that's why you had your crisis."

"Okay," he said after a while. "Let me think about that."

The Wrong Woman

I wanted to turn Warren's therapy back to his relationship with Judy. By now, after we had explored his childhood and his fantasies, I understood why he stayed away from his wife. It wasn't because he was too busy. Busy men still see their wives.

By the confused dream-logic of the unconscious, he had tried to turn the tables on his mother by turning the tables on his wife. "Leave me alone" is the unconscious message, delivered thirty years late to the wrong woman. Warren's unconscious had been interpreting his wife's desires as neediness and dependency. He wanted nothing to do with a seemingly needy dependent woman who reminded him of his mother. He didn't want to have to take care of her at the expense of himself, the way he had done as a boy.

A woman connected to this type of MEM needs to recognize this core reality: He is acting out with her the scene he couldn't enact with his mother. He demands that *his wife* tolerate his distance, because *his mother* wouldn't tolerate it. His busy schedule is not the reason he is unavailable. Figure 6-1 illustrates this dynamic.

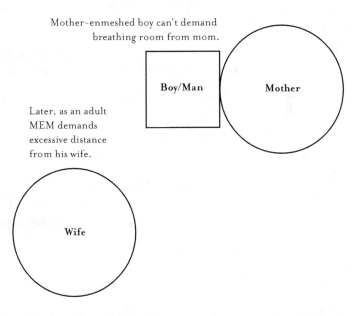

Couldn't Push Mom Away, Can Push You Away

Mother-enmeshed boy can't demand breathing room from mom.

Boy/Man   Mother

Later, as an adult MEM demands excessive distance from his wife.

Wife

Figure 6-1. A mother-enmeshed boy must tolerate excessive closeness from his mother. When the boy grows up, he demands that his wife be distant and tolerate what his mother wouldn't.

As I helped Warren see that he wanted to have more of a life, I also led him to understand that there was something more going on here than his own will. I would have liked to have arranged a group therapy experience for him, but high-profile clients are leery of the exposure of groups, and I knew from past experience that such a setting would not be right for him. Still, Warren was making good progress. He was aware of how his masturbation allowed him to avoid dealing with his life. He began to see how his solution to his enmeshment issues had become a problem.

He had continued to be actively enmeshed with his mother as an adult. He called often and went to see her when he could. He had remained her golden boy, even though he had become increasingly exhausted and resentful of the role. Now, finally, he was willing to set some boundaries with her. This was a new concept for him.

As Judy learned more of Warren's story, she eventually understood that he had been acting out with her his Disloyalty Bind with his mother. She understood that, but she still felt betrayed.

Their reconciliation required some negotiation. Couples counseling helped clear the air for them. As they differentiated their marital issues from their childhood wounds, what emerged was a true compatibility and affection, along with a need for some changes. Judy really did want to have him in her life, and he would have been lost without her. They were motivated to find common ground.

Warren was delighted once again to have a real woman in his arms, and he was also terrified. I worked with him to separate the past from the present. His adult conscious awareness didn't keep "little Warren," his mother's loyal servant, from being frightened. He "knew" his mother would view his success with this other woman as disloyalty, even though she was his wife. He was aware of a mounting anxiety when he was going to be with Judy, but he learned to manage this reaction as we worked on it.

Warren Sees His Mother

Warren had been having some encounters with his mother as he began to set boundaries with her. Before she had been just his nice old mother, who sometimes had too many needs for him to deal with. Now he could see her as demanding more than he should have to give. He would talk with her and then come to a session and tell me about it.

"I didn't say yes. This time I said, 'No. I can't help you, Mom,' and then she talked for five minutes about how sad that made her, and how she couldn't face the world if I didn't love her anymore."

He had many such encounters. He always covered his anxiety with humor, but over time he became less anxious. She persisted in telling him how sad he was making her, how she had nobody in the world except him, but he stuck by his guns. At long last he was done with the job of making her feel good.

Warren was astonished when I suggested that he share his sexual fantasies with Judy, but he eventually did, and that led to more intimacy between them. Over time he no longer needed his masturbation ritual as an escape.

Why Warren Will Never Be President

Warren has decided that he doesn't need to be president. Once he got in touch with who he was, he realized he didn't have to win his mother's approval and carry the burden of lifting her spirits. He didn't need to be the boss. He didn't need to be Number One. He had never needed it.

Today Warren has regained his close relationship with Judy, and they are both less depressed. He has given up his habit of escaping into fantasies. He is also less bound to do what his mother says. In particular, he is no longer compelled to be the ultimate hero for her. He has found some charities and causes that he can support outside the political arena, and he seems to be content.

Judy has learned to see herself as separate from Warren. She has become stronger and more assertive, and that was another challenge for Warren. He had to learn to see her demands as part of an adult process of negotiation.

When their marriage was role-defined, Judy and Warren knew what to do. Now they actually have to talk with each other. But he can appreciate her newfound clarity, and she accepts the need to be clear. Their connection deepened as they worked together.

Parallel, Apart, or Together

When Warren was a child, he lost himself in his mother's needs. After he grew up, he maintained and repeated the pain of his enmeshed childhood by demanding distance from his wife and by dulling and isolating himself with his daily masturbation to domination fantasies.

A couple does not remain half in growth and half trapped in the past. They live parallel lives or break apart or grow together. Warren and Judy wanted their connection and chose to grow together.

While some MEM are commitment phobic, another kind of MEM tends to feel committed and obligated within a few dates. Warren is one example, and Freddy in the next chapter is another. MEM are prone to specific problems as they try to connect with women. We look at these problems as we consider the theory of "courting," along with Freddy's story.

7 FREDDY HAS ANXIOUS SEX
The Lost Man

Freddy was feeling optimistic as he dressed for his "date" with his wife. The white linen jacket and light-blue cotton slacks helped. They made him feel sophisticated and in control. The new pills would solve his problem. His pal, Lou, had promised, and Lou was an M.D. Freddy imagined Angela looking at him with dreamy eyes of respect and satiation. They were going to the most expensive restaurant in town, then home to make love. He had planned it all.

Freddy was anxious throughout dinner. Angela was so cute in her minuscule black dress and pinned-up hair. Looking across the table at her, he was proud that she was his wife. She didn't say much; she let him talk. She smiled, but in that way she had where he couldn't tell what she was thinking. She had smiled like that when he had told her about Lou's pills.

The valet gave Angela "the look," but Freddy didn't mind. Tonight would be a new beginning. He eased his Explorer into the heavy traffic. He would show her.

In their bedroom, she casually dropped her dress and stood challengingly naked in her heels. Trembling, he kissed her. His plan had been to excuse himself for a minute to take the pills, but who could think at a time like this? She returned his kiss and pressed herself against him. His thrill was replaced by horror, as he felt himself giving way. Losing all sense of cool, he grabbed at himself through his slacks, but it was already too late. The stain showed up clearly. Angela was at first confused but, looking down, began to giggle. "Poor baby," she said. "I'm going to watch some TV." She pulled on her dress and left the room. Freddy stood alone, astonished by his familiar defeat. He imagined Angela all smashed and bloody in an auto crash. He savored the image.

I'm Tired of All This Shit

"I don't know why I'm here, Doc," Freddy began. "Lou thought you might be able to help me. I'm getting tired of all the shit in my life. I run the paint shop, and it's just one idiot mistake after the other. Listen to me when I tell you, Doc, those guys can't do anything right. I think they're just trying to mess things up. They don't care. They like things to mess up. I get blamed. They think it's funny. What do they care? They get paid no matter what. But it makes me look bad. I haven't had a fair evaluation in years. Bastards!"

This is significant, I thought. *Freddy is talking to me like I'm a drinking buddy. He doesn't provide any background or context. He calls me "Doc." This guy has trouble with authority and boundaries and relating to others. No wonder he is having a hard time.*

"It sounds like you're having some frustrations with people at work," I said. This set him off on another round of complaints. I kept my reactions very general and allowed him to vent. At some point, I tried to shift his attention from work with "Are there other relationships in your life that also give you trouble?"

"Well, yeah," he said. "My wife and my kids. They're a pain. They don't appreciate what all I do for them. Thank God I've got my buddy, Lou. If it wasn't for him, I don't know what I'd do. I'd probably shoot myself."

"Have you thought about shooting yourself?"

"No-o-o, that's just an expression."

"Have you been depressed?"

"Oh, yeah. Like everybody else, I get depressed sometimes. But it's no big deal."

"It looks like your friend, Lou, thinks a lot of you."

"He's just a buddy."

"Sounds like you have some concerns about your relationships. I'm sure I can be of some help to you. Why don't we get together again?"

Freddy became one of my most dependable clients. He liked to talk to me. He liked to vent, and he was lonely. Over time, his story emerged as an extreme case of the MEM syndrome.

Listening to Mom and Dad Argue

One night when Freddy was ten, he hid on the staircase to hear his parents argue about him.

"*He* listens to me," Sally said.

"What else can he do?" Peter replied, not looking up from the technical report he was reviewing.

"He listens to me, and you don't," she continued. "Thank God I have Freddy. Otherwise, I'd have nobody."

"I don't like him sleeping with you."

"*You're* not sleeping with me."

Peter didn't reply. It was a bad thing, his son so attached to his mother, but a convenient thing. "I've got to go back to the office," he said.

"I know," she said, sarcasm dripping. "You'll be working late."

He left, uninterested in the argument.

Freddy went down. "I just wanted to hug you good night," he said to his mother. She gave him a long, deep hug. "Can I sleep with you tonight, Mommy?" he asked, and was thrilled when she said yes.

The next day Freddy was "sick" and stayed home from school. "You really should do some homework," Sally said vaguely. "All right, Mommy," he replied, but he knew she wouldn't think about it again.

That night Sally ambushed Peter with the problems she was having with Freddy. "He isn't doing well in school. He won't do his homework," she said.

Peter talked to Freddy, but he was impatient, and it sounded like yelling to the boy. His mother was there, but she wasn't defending him. She was telling him to "shut up" and "listen to your father."

Freddy cried, as usual. His father called him a weakling and then stomped out, disgusted. Sally ran after him, leaving Freddy to wipe his tears by himself. She caught up with her husband, let him vent in the driveway, and then invited him back inside to share a glass of wine. Exhausted, Peter agreed. So that night he slept with his wife, and Freddy put himself to bed.

A Feeling of Inferiority

Freddy had an older brother and no other siblings. "My brother is a big shot, like the old man," Freddy told me, a little bitter but also admiring. Freddy had always felt inadequate and incompetent compared to his brother and father.

"Can you tell me how often you see your brother and what kinds of conversations you guys have?" I asked him. "Does he have the same kinds of problems with relationships?"

"Ah, no," Freddy replied. "He has lots of friends, and girl-friends too."

He saw his brother at family dinners and parties, but the brothers didn't get together one on one. The same with his father. And when they did meet, there still was always some kind of criticism directed toward Freddy. In fact, there was criticism coming from every important person in his life: his wife, his brother, his father.

His mother would sometimes come to his defense, but then she would scorn him and ridicule him along with the others. This two-faced behavior of his mother had been, and continued to be, particularly destructive for Freddy. I wondered what had happened in *her* childhood to make manipulation and betrayal a mainstay of her emotional vocabulary. This behavior pattern is typical of victims of sexual abuse. Freddy was unlikely to know about what kinds of abuse his mother had suffered as a child, but it was a possibility that I kept open to help with my analysis.

Freddy's sense of failure within his family carried over to work. He was a middle manager in the same company as his father and brother, but Freddy was without prospects of advancement. In contrast, his father was considered too indispensable to retire, in spite of his age, and his brother was in China, laying the foundation for the future of the company in Asia. Freddy was just a corporate bureaucrat, considered as interchangeable as any element of mass production, not respected by anybody.

Why Is Freddy Depressed?

Freddy knew he was dissatisfied, but he didn't have any conscious awareness that he was depressed. However, it was one of his major symptoms. It resulted from the fact that he tended to feel victimized in his relationships. I wanted to develop his awareness of the connection between how he was feeling and how his relationships made him feel. I wanted him to come to the realization "I feel helpless in my relationship, and therefore I feel depressed."

Devil Dad and Angel Mom

After discussing his brother, Freddy moved on to the theme of his father's bad treatment of his mother. I took the opportunity to ask him about his mother specifically.

MASKED DEPRESSION

Terrence Real, in his book I Don't Want to Talk About It: Overcoming the Secret Legacy of Male Depression, *notes that depression can show itself in men as irritability, aggression, anger, complaining, or acting out. Real suggests that both men and women look down on men who allow themselves to be seen as "weak" by admitting they feel depressed. Thus, it is "safer" to convert depression into other feelings. Depression in men, Real argues, often goes undiagnosed, while rage and aggression are often identified as male shortcomings.*

✎

"She was like all mothers," he said. "She cooked and cleaned. She stayed home and took care of me. She put up with my father's bullshit."

In light of all Freddy's problems, I doubted this was the whole story. Judging from his extreme inability to relate, his choice of the woman he married, coupled with his one-sided idealized version of his mother, I could deduce that young Freddy's relationship with his mother was not nurturing but destructive.

A person with healthy mothering might say "You know, there were good and bad things. I didn't like it when she did this, but I liked it when . . ." There would be a more balanced and realistic view. When a client presents to me these extremes—specifically, very dysfunctional adult behavior coupled with an idealized story of childhood—I know that there is a history of terrible damage being denied.

I took the threads he offered. "What kind of things did your mother have to put up with from your father?"

"He yelled at her. Mom said he was 'fooling around,' and that's why he didn't want to spend time with us. But still, she worked to keep the family together."

"How did witnessing your mother going through hell with your father affect you?"

"Sometimes it would bother me," he admitted, "when she would come to me to cry. I was upset to see her so unhappy."

"Sometimes she would get angry with me," Freddy then volunteered, "and I really felt awful about it." At last, he was offering a piece of his vulnerability.

"It sounds like you were bothered sometimes about your mother's crying. When she got angry, you found that difficult to take."

WHAT IS DENIAL?

Denial is the inability to correctly perceive an unacceptable or painful reality about ourselves or our parents or others. People who have been abused as children often idealize their childhoods. They may report "nothing" was wrong, when there was severe abuse. They are often "in denial."

✧

"Well, I guess so, but Dad . . ." And he continued on the theme of devil dad and angel mom. But the door had been opened to his feelings about his mother, and over the coming sessions he was willing to share more.

Eventually I could ask, "What were some of her criticisms of you? Tell me about those."

Without thinking, he said, "She'd say the same things to me that she said to my father. But sometimes I'd get it worse than him. It seemed like she would take it all out on me, and what was I supposed to do?"

"How did that make you feel?"

"I felt like I wasn't good enough. I could never please her."

This was important. His mother's criticism was a key component of his feeling helpless, and that helplessness was linked to his depression and his disengaged relationship with his wife. Even though his father and brother criticized him, too, his mother's contribution was much more fundamental.

How to Court a Woman

When Freddy was nineteen, he became infatuated with a stripper at a local club. She got pregnant, and he married her.

In marrying a stripper, he thought that he would live out a nonstop sexual fantasy. Reality hit hard. He was the type of impulsive naive MEM who declares loyalty and obligation without taking time to get to know the woman, to decide if she would actually be good for him. Angela could dance in front of men, where she stayed in control, but she couldn't be intimate. A man for her meant "audience," not "partner." Freddy married someone who wanted to play games and have affairs, but who lacked the capacity to care for him.

There is a natural progression of stages when two people are moving in the direction of love and commitment. Psychologists use the old-fashioned word "courting" for the process. Basically, a couple becomes closer and more committed and intimate over time, as they establish each other's suitability.

People who grow up in families where there is not a disruption in the normal stages of childhood development typically follow in adulthood a predictable sequence of stages in courting. The five stages are:

Stage 1. *Noticing.* Becoming interested in someone.

Stage 2. *Flirting.* Showing interest and worthiness to that person.

Stage 3. *Dating.* Getting to know the person.

Stage 4. *Intimacy.* Sharing at the deepest level. Sex may begin here.

Stage 5. *Commitment.* Pledging to an exclusive long-term bond, such as marriage.

MEM often exhibit the following types of dysfunctional courting patterns:

- Stage 1 only. Interest and noticing do not lead to contact but rather to fantasies. Sam in Chapter 5 has this tendency.

- Stages 1, 2, and 3, but not Stages 4 or 5. He never sticks around. He is always seeking another woman. This is the pattern of the womanizer, like Doug (Chapter 2) before therapy.

- Stages 1, 2, 3, and 4, but not Stage 5. Here is the MEM who just can't take that last step to commitment. Sonny in Chapter 1 was like this before therapy.

- Stage 1 and then Stage 5, without going through Stages 2, 3, and 4. In this pattern, the man feels loyal and committed too quickly, before he can properly decide if the woman is in his best interest. Freddy did this with Angela, and Warren (Chapter 6), who committed when he was too young to make such a decision, did it too.

The goal of courting is choosing wisely, followed by commitment. Successful courting requires the freedom to offer increasing amounts of commitment at the different stages: Stage 1: You look attractive. Stage 2: I like you. Stage 3: I want to go out with you. Stage 4: I want to be exclusive with you, and I want you to be exclusive with me. Stage 5: I want to be with you through thick and thin and work through difficulties, and I want you to be committed to me.

A Wife Like Mom

Inspired by his stories about his mother and father, I asked, "Are there ways in which your wife is critical of you or makes you feel inadequate?"

"Yeah," Freddy said. "She's always bitching at me and comparing me to these guys at work. I'm certain that she's doing something too," he added. "I confront her, and we have these fights. I know she's lying, but I can't get her to admit it." So "suddenly" it just sort of poured out. After nine months of talking to me and not revealing the pain in his marriage, he was admitting that he really felt hurt and diminished with his wife.

What I was seeing, as he described his marriage, was his emotional template, forged by his true relationship with his mother, so different from the "she was an angel" fairy tale. His marriage followed that template: He was diminished and emasculated, used when necessary and put off when no longer needed. His unconscious had made this choice. Here was where his current sense of being helpless came from. Here was why he saw himself as a victim, and it explained his anger and frustration. He felt helpless to do anything about this woman who had power over him, originally his mother but now her replacement, his wife.

Freddy's wife had married him for his money, and she expected to have fun with it without having to bother much with him. She used criticism and contempt to keep him off guard. His teenage children's natural adolescent contempt was confirmed and enhanced by his wife's scornful opinion of him. But with all this, Freddy had another problem.

Anxious Sex

At some point, in the midst of a typical venting about how unfair people were to him, he let slip that he hadn't had sex in years.

"I know it's because she's going out on me," he said. "I'm never enough for her."

"How do you mean?"

Freddy looked at his shoe. "You know how it sometimes

happens too quickly?" he said. "She doesn't cut me any slack about it either."

"That must be very difficult. It's tough to have that happen and then have your wife be critical about it."

"Yeah, you're damn right it is. . . ." Then he realized what he was revealing and tried to brush it off. "It's no big deal," he said. He didn't want to go there. That was okay. We would get back to it.

As I learned more, I could piece together his sexual history. Freddy was the guy whose style of courting was to go directly from noticing to commitment, and his idea of noticing was looking at Angela dancing naked on stage. When she showed an interest in him, he immediately idealized her and felt committed.

By the time Freddy had been married to Angela a few months, he had a chronic problem with premature ejaculation. This condition directly reflected how he had felt as a child with his mother: frightened and excited, overanxious and over-aroused. After several years of marriage, he generally couldn't even get an erection. His sexual response was a combination of the various forces that competed in him. Being close to a woman meant ridicule, scorn, engulfment, and entrapment. This was his most primitive response to his mother as a child, evoked in adulthood by his marriage. But even though his body was shutting down as a response to this danger, he felt obligated to stay with Angela, because he had transposed his Disloyalty Bind to her, as a stand-in for his mother. Finally, because his mother had been his only source of affirmation when he was little, as inconsistent as this had been, he waited for what crumbs of kindness he could glean from his wife. He believed he had no alternatives. He couldn't let himself know how he felt, because of his Lost Identity. He lacked the courage to act, because of his low self-esteem.

Freddy also worried that his inability to perform with Angela meant he was gay. Many men who have been psychologically emasculated like Freddy have this worry. However, if Freddy had been gay, he would have had a primary interest in men, which he did not. Emasculation doesn't indicate orientation. It reflects a sense of inadequacy that gets displaced onto sexual performance, a condition that affects gay and straight men alike.

What Should Freddy Do?

As Freddy came to understand the devastating effect his marriage was having on his spirit, he asked me what he should do about it.

"I want to help you continue to strengthen your own awareness," I told him, "so that you can be more confident when you interact with your wife, because it sounds like she's contributing to your distress.

"You could choose to go into marriage counseling as an adjunct to what we are doing," I ventured, "and begin to discuss your issues with her. However, I think you should wait to do that. The time to start marriage counseling is when you feel you can hold on to your own truth. Then, even if you're fearing retaliation from your wife, you will be able to say how things look to you. Your truth needs to be more important to you than pleasing your wife."

Strippers

Now we were entering into the heart of his therapy, what we had worked two years to achieve. The goal was to get him to see that he was living out a template forged in the past, and, if he wanted to change his life, he was going to have to look at that template. I asked him directly if his feelings toward his wife were like those he had when he was a little boy. He began to acknowledge that he had felt this anxiety and hopelessness with his mother. It was then that he had his first hard-won moment of intuitive insight.

He said, "You know, my mother used to take off her clothes in front of me sometimes. And I'd get a boner and try to hide it, and I'd be blushing, and she would tease me about it. It's the way I felt when I first watched Angela dance. She teased me too. She got off on making me squirm."

So here he achieved a turning point: He'd linked together his relationships with his mother and with his wife. His relationship with his mother was seductive, enmeshing, and involuntary, and it left him vulnerable to a crude seduction in adulthood. Angela dancing was seductive enough to evoke the pattern his mother had established. He had spent his childhood taking care of his dishonest, seductive mother. She undressed in front of him, unconcerned about any damage he might suffer and enjoying the attention she was commanding from her son. These sexual overtones in his relationship with his mother were significant. She had crossed the boundary from enmeshment to sexual abuse. Boys can be sexually abused by women, even though abuse by men has been reported more frequently. See *Beyond Betrayal* by Richard Gartner for a more complete discussion.

Of course, when Freddy realized what he'd said, he backed away.

"This is too much for me," he said in a kind of panic. "No Freudian shit for me. I don't want to have sex with my mother. That's ridiculous."

Because I had established some trust over our two years together, and he had built up some resources, I was able to say "Let's stay with this for a minute. It sounds like you may have discovered something. Can you tell me more about what it felt like to be around your mother when she undressed?" He didn't object, and I went on, "It sounds like your mother left you feeling excited, diminished, emasculated, criticized. . . . It's like the way your wife, and all other women, make you feel."

And so he understood and felt the truth of it. His relationship with his wife was like the one he had had with his mother.

Freddy had an above-average IQ, but his intelligence had been limited by the need to support his denial. Now that he had negotiated with his unconscious a loosening of its defense against the old danger, his intelligence could help him out. It could make sense of what he'd been experiencing. His unconscious had reached an accord with his conscious, which is what a "moment of intuitive insight" in therapy is.

After this session, for the first time in his life, Freddy became truly reflective. He had some further moments of insight. His mind had begun to heal itself, a self-sustaining process that would continue. His need to defend against the truth was no longer controlling his mind. From now on he would be inclined to reflect on his life rather than avoid thinking about it.

Relationships Evolve or They Die

Freddy was starting to set boundaries with his mother. He wasn't so ruled by guilt and the Disloyalty Bind. He didn't feel obligated to see her when he didn't want to. He didn't confront her, but he didn't listen to her complaining about his father anymore either. We practiced what he would say: "I don't really want to listen to this anymore. Please stop or I've got to go."

Freddy started having lunch with his father occasionally. He didn't expect much affection, but he wanted to claim his rightful place as his father's son. He wanted to show that he could face his father without having to explain himself or feel inadequate. There were no intimate discussions between them. I had cautioned Freddy not to expect any.

Freddy was now ready for marriage counseling. Angela agreed to go with him, because it wasn't a problem for her. She did it as a favor. She felt sorry for him. The new Freddy surprised her.

He told her, "I don't need a nasty marriage. We either make things better between us, or I will have to make things better by myself."

Angela was stunned. He had threatened divorce before, but now he wasn't threatening. He was being matter-of-fact. And Angela had to deal with the fact that she could no longer provoke him like she once did.

He told her, "If you don't stop having affairs, I will divorce you now. If you want to stop having affairs and come into therapy with me, I'm willing to see if we can work something out."

She denied the affairs, and he said, "I'm not going to argue with you about it. I know what I know." Freddy could hold on to his truth now. Now he could take a position with her.

Angela went to a few counseling sessions with him, but she showed little willingness or ability to be insightful about herself. She blamed him for their troubles. Freddy would still get drawn into it for a time, but he knew now that it wasn't true. He filed for divorce. When therapy is successful, relationships either change or end. Partners come together on the therapeutic journey, or they part.

Angela forced an angry divorce. Freddy was fearful but not intimidated, and got a lawyer who was willing to fight for him. The old Freddy would have just given Angela everything to avoid a fight.

In the middle of these battles, Freddy quit his job, giving up fifteen years of seniority to find something that was more meaningful. He thought he would do some traveling. He wasn't sure what he would do after that, but he would find something that made sense to him.

Freddy also made a more definite attempt to establish a relationship with his children. They were contemptuous of him, but he was calmly persistent in working to see them separately and have them see him with their own eyes, not the eyes of their mother.

Freddy changed his life to reflect who he really was and what he really wanted to do. He had recovered his courage and his compass. The world was his to explore.

Memories as Problems

The competitive drama with his father that Freddy was forced to endure goes far beyond the natural competition between father and son. The source of Freddy's gender identification—his father—was chronically angry with him and scornful. Under the circumstances, he could not help but think that he was not worthy of his father's love. A boy is terrified if he succeeds in winning his mother from his father. His father then becomes a source of danger to him, and the boy is cut off from a vital link to his masculinity.

Freddy's problem with sexual performance was a memory of the overeroticized, confusing, dangerous relationship with his mother, titillating as well as threatening, overwhelming with the weight of adult authority over a child. He had no say in it. He wanted her but was afraid to want her. Later, in incidents with his father, he felt rejected. All of this was part of his memory. When he was with his wife, the threat of rejection terrified him and interfered with his sexual performance, which provoked further rejection. His premature ejaculation was a way to get the encounter over with quickly and minimize his fear and anxiety.

There is nothing our society would call brutal in little Freddy's childhood, no hitting, no starvation, no running ragged in the streets. Freddy wasn't raised in a shack, but his emotional world was worse than a shambles. It was a war zone, shot full of mean words and sarcasm, scorn and competition, lying and betrayal. The wounds from this war had stayed festering: rages "forgotten" but not healed, faults implied but not specified, unexplained cold shoulders. Adults who don't take responsibility and apologize are implicitly blaming the child. And the child has no choice but to accept the blame.

All of the men in this book have been exploited by their mothers for emotional support. Freddy's mother didn't just use him for an inappropriate adultlike friendship. She used him in a way that would be harmful to an adult, with lies and betrayals. To a child, it was not just harmful. It was devastating.

❧

Mother-son enmeshment skews loyalty, disrupts identity, cripples self-esteem, breeds guilt, and generates all the other symptoms we have so far considered. In particular, it disables a MEM's ability to leave destructive relationships. In the next chapter, Arthur can't leave his job and move forward in his life. He is loyal to the company that is betraying him.

8 WHY DO MOTHER-ENMESHED MEN STRUGGLE TO BE TRUE TO THEMSELVES?

Betrayed by Enmeshment

Arthur worked for a major automotive parts supplier. He'd had a fairly reasonable lower-middle-class standard of living, but that was ending. Arthur had been forced to take a 20 percent cut in pay. He had a wife, three children, two dogs, a mortgage, and car payments. He could no longer pay his bills.

I had a chance to talk with Arthur socially at a gathering of people I had known in high school. He was anxious, angry, and resentful. He felt betrayed. But he didn't plan to find a new job. His sense of betrayal did not diminish his sense of loyalty to the company.

Ben was also at this gathering. He had switched jobs a few years before, from something in manufacturing to social work. He was trying to convince Arthur that he should make a career change too.

"You can get some training," Ben said. "Learn to do something different. I did it."

"I know," Arthur said. "But I just can't quit my job. I've got a lot of seniority. I don't want to give that up."

This response got Ben fuming. "You're probably going to lose your job! What does seniority matter?"

Arthur insisted he couldn't leave. "Things might get better," he said. "Things might pick up, and we'll get our overtime again."

"It looks like you're being loyal in a situation that doesn't warrant it," I said.

"Yeah, I know, but I can't leave. We'll see what happens."

"Arthur," Ben said, "the handwriting is on the wall. That company isn't going to give you what you want. You'll be lucky to have a job two years from now. They're going to go bankrupt. They'll create a new company and offer you ten dollars an hour, if you're lucky. The executives are demanding concessions from the union while they walk away with millions for themselves. Why should you be loyal to them?"

"You're right," Arthur said, but his agreement seemed to be only an attempt not to hear more.

"You need to help yourself before it's too late," I said, backing up Ben.

"What could I do at another company? I'm just going to have to wait and hope for the best."

Stuck Being Loyal

Inappropriate loyalty is a characteristic of mother-enmeshed men. Although he was never a client, I learned enough about Arthur to believe that he was a MEM. For example, his first wife had left him, saying that his mother had too much influence over his life. Although his new family seems to be doing fine, his relationship with his work follows the pattern of MEM. His loyalty to work was the same one-sided loyalty he had with his mother.

Arthur's story is a classic illustration of how a MEM gets

stuck, and it is also a good example of how the template of en-meshment can be evoked with respect to life opportunities. We've already considered the dynamic of a man's enmeshed re-lationship with his mother preventing him from committing to his partner. Sonny, Doug, and Sam from earlier chapters are all good examples. However, the template can be transposed, so that the company plays the role of the mother and new oppor-tunities play the role of the girlfriend/partner/wife. In this vari-ation on the theme of mother-son enmeshment, the MEM is stuck with an abusive company, and he has trouble even consid-ering leaving for something better. A MEM's loyalty serves oth-ers; he has trouble acting for himself.

When this MEM thinks about leaving, he feels terrible. "I can't leave. No one else would want me. I'm not good enough." This is the voice of low self-worth, holding him in place with shame. "I shouldn't do this. I'm wrong to do this. I should stay here." This is the Disloyalty Bind, holding him in place with guilt. Even in the face of overt betrayal, the MEM can't leave. He can't go after what he wants.

Patrick Carnes, in his book *The Betrayal Bond,* states that people who are betrayed as children tend to stay with, and try harder in, abusive relationships rather than leave them, creating "betrayal bonds." This general principle goes beyond mother-son enmeshment to a wide variety of emotional trauma. How-ever, MEM are strongly driven to declare loyalty and make attachments in relationships where betrayal is inherent. Then, because of their dependency and early programming created by the enmeshment, they are unable to extract themselves from these destructive connections. This behavior pattern has al-ready been illustrated in Chapter 7. Freddy, the lost man, im-petuously married a woman who was bound to betray him.

Freddy had a childhood with extreme elements of emotional violence, but all MEM childhoods are betraying to some degree. The next box summarizes the typical elements found in the childhoods of most MEM.

CHARACTERISTICS OF A MEM'S CHILDHOOD

1. His mother keeps him close to her.

2. His mother often intrudes into his privacy, even when he protests.

3. His mother tells him about her anger with her husband, her sexual frustration, or other adult matters.

4. He often escorts his mother to social functions. He is her little companion.

5. Grown-ups often comment on how "well behaved" he is, or they say he is a "little adult."

6. His mother discourages activities that take him away from her, including sports and play with other children, especially girlfriends.

7. He sometimes avoids going to school or going out so that he can stay home, close to his mother.

8. His mother makes decisions for him and determines his interests without asking him.

9. His mother has few outside interests or adult friends. He is the predominant focus of her life.

10. His mother is unhappy in her marriage and a martyr. He has become the person she can count on.

11. He takes on in his own personality the same depression and social isolation of his mother.

12. His father is either absent or ineffective, while the son becomes the man of the house.

13. His mother discourages any connection with his father.

14. He feels abandoned by or distant from his father.

15. He feels scorn and contempt toward his father.

The Disloyalty Bind and the Lost Identity

Arthur agreed that he should leave and then he said that he couldn't leave. This contradiction is explained by understanding the workings of the Disloyalty Bind. Once a man is controlled by the Disloyalty Bind, an unending source of guilt tells him that he *should not commit* to a new opportunity or a new woman. But the trap is even more powerful. The Disloyalty Bind evokes low self-worth as well as guilt. Because the MEM has lost his identity, he is willing to act the role of subservient loyal employee out of his False Self while neglecting the needs of his True Self. He will complain plenty but not leave. This cascade of damage is shown in Figure 8-1.

When the little boy wanted to move away from his mother, as all little boys eventually do, his mother pulled him back, implicitly telling him he was bad for wanting to leave Mommy. But he felt a fundamental need to leave, so he was forced to conclude that he was fundamentally bad for wanting to leave. The guilt of "I should not want to leave" has generated "I am bad for wanting to leave." Guilt is joined by shame, the shame is manifested as low self-worth, and now the man feels that he *cannot commit* to a new opportunity or woman. The double bondage of *should not* and *cannot* makes the MEM's commitment phobia doubly entrenched. But also he has a Lost

Enmeshment Stifles the Life Force

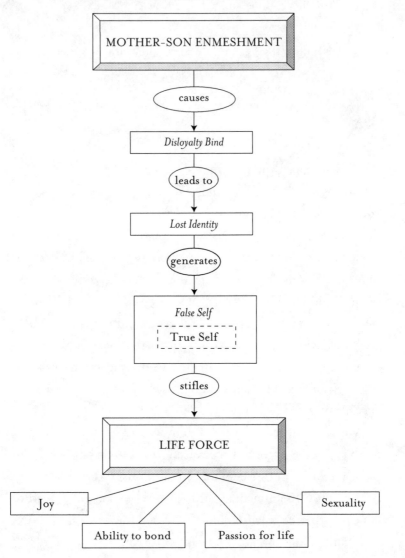

Figure 8-1. A MEM develops a False Self to act out the "roles" required of him. Meanwhile, his True Self becomes smothered and suppressed. As a consequence, his life force is stifled.

Identity. He must let go of "who he is" to adopt the role of "who he must be." When he loses his identity, he adopts a False Self—who lives only to please his mother and by extension all others—while his True Self is smothered and neglected.

A MEM like Arthur seems so indecisive because he is only vaguely aware of what he wants while at the same time he is clearly aware of "what is expected of him." Because his deeply entrenched Lost Identity supports his False Self at the expense of his True Self, a MEM cannot marshal his own will and determination to act in his own best interest. He cannot break through the inappropriate loyalty. He has no hard edge with which to take action. He doesn't seem to have the ability to endure the uncertainty of transitions to move ahead in his life. This is the essence of the "neglect of self" and the "people-pleasing" symptoms of the MEM. He is eager to help others; he cannot help himself. He commonly medicates the pain of this denial and loss via alcohol, drugs, food, or sex, leading him to addictions. The sexuality of a MEM is often imprinted with pathways designed for escape rather than connection. As we have already seen, all these symptoms are generated by the enmeshment dynamic.

False Self and True Self

Let me clarify the distinction between the True Self and the False Self. The "True Self" refers to a capacity of a person to be aware and express a full range of feelings (including emotional pain) and to use this awareness to navigate through life. For the True Self, core beliefs and values don't depend on somebody else's opinions. The "False Self" is about the repression and denial of unacceptable feelings, needs, wants, and desires in order to maintain approval and secure love at all costs. Some of the consequences of a MEM living in the False Self are:

- Difficulty identifying and expressing feelings
- Difficulty with intimacy
- Perfectionism
- Rigidness
- Difficulty making decisions
- Extremes of being overly dependent and then overly independent
- Needing other people's approval to feel good about himself

These aspects of a MEM's behavior all result from his desperate need to play the roles assigned to him.

What's Wrong with Roles?

Everyone modifies actions and responses to be in accord with societal norms. Work enforces codes of behavior on many people while on the job. Participants in sports play according to the rules. But in the psychological sense, "roles" are severely limiting ways of living that inhibit the natural development of a person's identity, including emotional responses and choices. "Role players" identify strongly with their roles; often they don't realize that they are *not* their roles. They have lost the sense of how they truly feel and who they really are. They have become "role defined."

A role is an outside presentation to the world that does not reflect the True Self. Roles enforce a rigid response to life that would otherwise be more naturally variable. Families are often containers and reinforcers of roles that are sustained by the denial of feelings, the denial of reality, and escape into numbing comforts. When a MEM attunes to Mom and sacrifices his needs to serve hers, he learns a role that he takes with him for the rest of his life. He thinks the role is his identity, when, in fact, it is an expression of the False Self. I have identified four roles that MEM often fall into: the Hero, the Caretaker, Mr. Fix-it, and the Charmer.

The Hero

The hero knows he is special, and he expects to save the day. Given an elevated position in the family by his mother, he's often resented by his siblings. We see him always in the spotlight, looking perfect, winning all the prizes. The hero tends to be controlling rather than placating, and he looks for a woman that he can dominate and feel superior to. Warren in Chapter 6 is a hero.

The Caretaker

The caretaker is always trying to help others with their problems. Tending to identify himself with a profession, such as doctor or therapist or lawyer, he can relate to people only through his role. He attaches himself to people with problems—in particular, women with problems—because he's taken his role as his mother's confidant into his adult life. He had to listen to all her problems, and now he listens to everyone's problems. Father Mark in Chapter 4 is a caretaker. Sonny in Chapter 1 is a cross between the hero and the caretaker.

Mr. Fix-it

Mr. Fix-it tries to escape the emotional trap of enmeshment by focusing on technical problems. For example, he might identify himself with the role of engineer or scientist. When his problems do involve people, his main focus is not necessarily on listening to them, as has been the case with some of my clients who were doctors and surgeons. Sam in Chapter 5 is this kind of MEM.

The Charmer

The charmer becomes the ideal companion his mother longed for: a charming, savvy boyfriend. He acts out the role endlessly with many women, not seeing that his life is a repetition of what happened with his mother. Doug in Chapter 2 is a charmer.

∽

When a MEM is stuck in a role, he cannot be authentic. He has to be loyal to the role. A MEM's childhood role was to take care of his mother. He was her hero or her caretaker or her Mr. Fix-it or her charmer. He had to suppress his True Self to become the role. As an adult, he is divorced from his True Self, and he is committed to his False Self, that is, his role. The caretaker might function well in a caretaking job like therapist, doctor, or nurse, but his role doesn't do him much good in his personal life. He's likely to pick as his partners and friends people who need to be taken care of. He cannot "be himself" with them, and usually he doesn't find much satisfaction in his relationships.

The Power of the Unconscious Mind

The Disloyalty Bind and the Lost Identity are such dominant controllers of a MEM because they are operating from his unconscious. This doesn't mean just that he is unaware of them. The unconscious works at a more primitive level than the conscious mind. It often "thinks" it is responding to danger, and it overrides the conscious mind to compel a life-or-death response. It is so sure it is right that it is willing to force the MEM to repeat patterns that get him into trouble, or it inhibits actions that will make his life better.

We can now consider a new expanded interpretation of "commitment phobia": The MEM can't leave a bad deal for a good deal. When it's romance, the good deal is the woman; when it's occupational, the good deal is a better work opportunity; when it is about life in general, the good deal is any life-affirming change that the MEM can't pursue because he feels too bound by guilt and shame, too indecisive because of his Lost Identity and low self-worth, and too numb to his own needs and too unable to marshal his own resources.

The Therapeutic Journey

The losses to a MEM continue to get worse over time. If he avoids treatment, there is less and less of his "identity" to work with, fewer and fewer resources that can be brought to bear, and more and more shame. When I met Arthur, he didn't have many resources left. I realized then that, if he didn't face his Disloyalty Bind, he'd never be able to make things better for himself. We all urged him to consider changes that would improve his life. He agreed with us, but I sensed he might no longer have the inner strength to act on that knowledge.

Unless the MEM seeks help, the damage to his life force is powerful and permanent. By "life force" I mean a man's capacity for joy, his ability to bond, his passion for life, and his sexuality. When he follows the recovery strategies and therapy programs described in Part Two and Part Three, a MEM can learn to live in the present without fighting ghosts from the past. His capacity for intimacy, connection, and trust will increase significantly.

However, if he does not address his issues, he will find himself trapped and frustrated and without options. He will never have the intimate relationships he longs for. Instead, his sexuality may be trapped forever in fantasies and addictions. It's likely he will drink too much, use drugs, become addicted to television, lose himself in cybersex, or eat beyond reason. He will be lonely all the time. If he is lucky, his work will be one area of success. But for a MEM like Arthur, success even there is doubtful.

As summarized in Figure 8-1, enmeshment causes the False Self, and the False Self stifles the life force. A therapist helping a MEM understands that the power of the enmeshment dynamic must be countered by bringing the client to a realization of what has happened to him, so that he can build new healthier core beliefs and life habits.

∽

Figure 8-2 summarizes Part One, by showing the MEM from Chapters 1 to 7 along with their principal characteristics and symptoms. Part Two will focus on the fundamentals of healing.

Healing is always possible. With healing, a MEM can learn to live in the present without fighting ghosts from the past. He can develop his capacity for intimacy, connection, and trust. Without healing, the MEM's sexuality will remain trapped in fantasies and compulsions. His intimate relationships will be unsatisfying, or he may avoid intimate relationships entirely.

Many of my clients have been able to shake loose from the domination of their enmeshment. They are no longer isolated

MEM in Part One

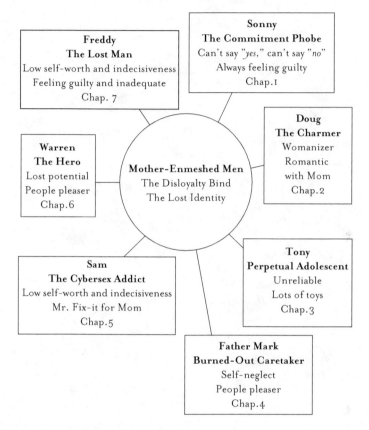

Figure 8-2. Various types of MEM give emphasis to certain symptoms over others, as indicated.

from themselves, and they are no longer living the pretense of their False Selves. The True Self is waiting to reemerge. The opportunities of the life force are never lost.

PART TWO

How Can You Heal?

9 BECOMING AWARE
Making the Unconscious Visible

Are you a mother-enmeshed man? Or is your partner one? This chapter begins with a questionnaire to help you decide. Answer each question (or have him answer each question) with a yes or a no. The first intuitive response—the gut reaction—is usually best.

Are You a Mother-Enmeshed Man?

1. Do you often feel preoccupied about your mother's unhappiness in her life?
2. Do you think of your mother as perfect or a martyr?
3. Have you ever felt obliged to fix, take care of, or get involved in your mother's problems?
4. Are you the most important person in your mother's life, or have you been in the past?
5. Do you often escort your mother to social functions, or did you do this in the past?
6. Have you felt engulfed, smothered, or intruded on by your mother?
7. Do interactions with your mother often leave you feeling guilty that you are not doing enough for her?

8. Does your mother put down or criticize your girlfriend or wife?

9. Are you distant from your father?

10. Do you often feel scorn or contempt toward your father?

11. Are you more comfortable relating to women than men?

12. Have you felt controlled, smothered, or entrapped in many of your romantic relationships?

13. Do you often put other people's feelings and needs first before you own?

14. Do you often feel guilty when pursuing your own wants or needs?

15. Has it happened to you more than once that you walked away from a romantic relationship even though you suspected it could have been good for you?

16. Have you been overly loyal in a bad situation or destructive relationship?

17. Do you often feel anxious when you and your partner are physically separated?

18. Have you felt depressed or helpless in attempting to positively impact your life?

19. Have you struggled to make life decisions that you felt others might make more easily?

20. Have you felt like you have failed to live out your heart's true desire?

Enmeshment and its consequences occur on a continuum. Some MEM are more enmeshed than others. The more questions with a "yes" answer, the more a significant a problem with mother-son enmeshment is indicated. If you decide to consult with a therapist or counselor (see Chapter 10), then the answers here would make a good starting point for your consultation.

No clinically established cutoff scores have been established yet for this questionnaire.

Your Unconscious Mind

MEM keep repeating their mistakes: dating the wrong women, not committing to the right women, quitting good jobs, sticking with bad jobs, losing weight and regaining more, throwing away their money, getting hooked on alcohol or drugs or cybersex or television. And the people who know them ask: "His first wife was wonderful for him, and he left her and married someone else. Now they're getting divorced. What is he looking for? What does he think he'll find?" Or "He's got so much intelligence and talent. How can he stay in that dead-end job where they don't respect him?"

The explanation is simple. The MEM's unconscious mind is enforcing his Disloyalty Bind. Making bad choices keeps him dependent on, and loyal to, his mother. This is not a conscious thought process. In fact, his conscious mind would reject the odd chain of analogies that the unconscious finds compelling. A wife is not a mother. A job is not a mother. But the dream logic of the unconscious is not bound by sequential reasoning. It reacts to its sense of how things feel.

Being so strongly influenced by his unconscious, the MEM finds it difficult to stay in the present. For example, let's consider David, a client of mine. Often, when David's wife asked him for something, he would have an immediate unconscious reaction from the past: "Here it is again. Here's another demand from my mother, and I don't want to deal with it. I don't want to talk about it. I want to run away."

But after David had become more aware, he knew where that fear came from. Then he could say to himself, "Let me

UNCONSCIOUS TEMPLATES

The unconscious mind can be provoked in situations that are parallel to those in a person's past. When this happens, it may generate some of the feelings and strong emotions from the past, such as fear and anger. It has the power to override the conscious mind when it perceives a crisis. Childhood trauma can distort the unconscious mind's understanding of what is a crisis and what is not. For a MEM, even a minor request for a connection might provoke a flood of fear and anger over the prospect of being "trapped again."

think about this for a minute. Is my wife making a reasonable request that is pushing the buttons of my unconscious? Or is she asking for too much, and do I need to stand up for myself?" Being aware allowed David to navigate the complexity of relationships. Without awareness, he was at the mercy of his unconscious beliefs and responses.

The Split Brain

Brain science supports the realization that people are not aware of all their mental processes. Using brain scans that show which areas of the brain are active during a variety of activities, scientists have observed that some of our actions are unconscious, particularly when we are under stress. When we are faced with an emotionally or physically stressful situation, the right hemisphere of the brain, which includes the unconscious, becomes active. See the box "Right Brain, Left Brain."

The complex interactions between the brain and behavior have been documented in a vast body of scientific and medical research. See, for example, the work by Dr. Alan Schore listed in the bibliography.

We think we know why we do things, but in times of crisis we do not. Under stress the more fundamental, intuitive, and reactive side of the brain is in charge. For example, if a MEM's girlfriend wants him to take a step that suggests further commitment in their relationship, he might overreact by feeling he's being trapped and overwhelmed. He might get angry. He might withdraw. His right brain "knows" there is danger and acts to save him. Thus, the unconscious protective mechanism can respond to a current situation as if it were an old toxic situation of the past.

RIGHT BRAIN, LEFT BRAIN

Generally speaking, the brain is divided into two "hemispheres"—right and left. The left hemisphere is typically associated with analytic and reasoned thoughts. Often it's the part of the brain that guides conscious awareness. The other parts of the brain, including the right hemisphere, support emotional responses and what we refer to as the unconscious mind. Speaking of the "emotional unconscious right brain" and the "logical conscious left brain" is a convenient shorthand, commonly used.

What does right-brain "knowing" mean? The right brain doesn't "know" in the detached pictorial or verbal way of the left brain. Rather, the right brain knows by reexperiencing a past situation in a vivid experiential, intuitive, and sensual way. The right brain doesn't *observe* the scene; it is *in* the scene. The request for a minor commitment by David's wife once felt to

David like entrapment and engulfment by his mother. He was there with his mother, and he reacted "without thinking" to the danger he felt. That feeling would override David's left-brain awareness that his wife is not his mother.

However, as the MEM becomes more aware of his unconscious responses, he can use his left-brain awareness and "reason with" his very protective right brain. Then he can correct his first reaction and respond more reasonably.

Acting as His Mother's Agent

Once I was teaching a series of classes at a treatment program for alcoholic and addicted priests. My class on mother-son enmeshment was called "Over Mothered and Under Fathered." As I presented my material, I could sense an unease building among some of the twenty-five priests in the room. Finally, one of them raised his hand. It was Father Paul.

"Oh, yeah," he said. "Now that you're talking about it, do you know about the survey that they did out at some East Coast diocese? They found out that a big percentage of the priests leaving the priesthood did it within two years after their mothers died."

The whole room went silent. I waited. Then several of the other priests objected. They seemed upset and offended, as if we shouldn't even be talking about priests and their mothers. Later that day, Father Paul let me know that a delegation from the class was circulating a petition complaining about me and my class. I wondered what would happen when that petition went to the treatment program leadership.

In the scene from *Psycho* described in Chapter 1, as soon as Norman Bates realizes that Marion might get between him and his mother, he decides to kill her. These priests with their petition also wanted to "kill the messenger." An unconscious part of a MEM aligns and identifies with his mother and becomes her agent. This agent acts to destroy, dismiss, or reject anything that gets in the way of the enmeshed mother-son connection. Moreover, it acts outside the awareness and will of the MEM. The strong reaction of these priests made me realize what a taboo subject mother-son enmeshment can be for everyone. Fortunately, in spite of the petition, the head of the treatment program didn't ask me to make any changes in my class.

Here is another case story that illustrates the "agent for mother" idea. Jim had played the role of his mother's surrogate husband since he was a little boy. When he was an adolescent, he started having girlfriends. His mother habitually criticized them, so he didn't keep any. As an adult, Jim came to me with a long history of anger at women, womanizing, and sexual compulsions. During therapy, at some point he got it. "Oh, my God," he said, "I use the same criticisms on the women in my life now that my mother used on my girlfriends." It was one of those aha! moments of intuitive insight. *He had become the voice of his mother.* The women coming into his life were bumping into what he had never resolved. He needed to get rid of them, because it's either *I'm loyal to Mom* or *I'm loyal to myself,* and being loyal to himself raised too much guilt. This was the Disloyalty Bind in action. So Jim eliminated the threat that produced the bad feelings: The girlfriends had to go. And one way to get them to go was to criticize them, the same way his mother had.

When somebody begins to interfere with a MEM's relationship with his mother, the MEM acts as his "mother's agent" to preserve the relationship. Examples of such interference include my teaching the "Over Mothered and Under Fathered" class, Marion in *Psycho* innocently suggesting to Norman that his mother might be mistreating him, and the girlfriends of my client, Jim. The MEM's mother doesn't even have to be around anymore. Mom could be across the country or in the house next door or dead. It doesn't matter. The MEM's mother's demand for loyalty has been internalized in the MEM's unconscious as the Disloyalty Bind. He automatically reacts on her behalf. He defends his enmeshed relationship, even though he is bound up by it and even though he consciously would like to leave it. He is loyal in spite of the cost to him.

The Left Brain Idealizes History; the Right Brain Acts It Out

The next scenario has happened frequently in my practice: I am working with somebody who grew up in what I later discover is an extremely abusive family. But at first the client says that his childhood was great. The family was loving. There were no problems. And this is in cases where there was severe violence in the family. When a person comes to see me with a history of serious emotional issues—addictions, affairs, phobias—my many years of clinical experience suggest that the stories of a "wonderful childhood" cannot be true.

How do I, as a therapist, get through this wall of denial? It is basically by asking for details, after the client trusts me enough to let me press a little. I say, "Would you change anything about your childhood, if you could go back and rewrite your history?" Typically, my client says "No," and then, "Well, yeah," and then the truth starts being revealed. After a while I'm asking, "What was that like, when your father pulled out the belt?" Prior to that everything in his childhood had been perfect every time I asked. I will also say, "Tell me how things were good. Did you have a lot of affection and love? How did you know you were loved? What kinds of expressions of love do you remember?" In abusive families, there is often little love or affection. The client might say, "I know they loved me. They just didn't show it." I am gently persistent: "How did you know? What did they do to let you know you were loved?" And perhaps another time: "What were the highlights of your childhood, the parts you liked the most?" Now some reality begins to enter. The denial gradually gives way.

But why does the MEM who grows up in a family with severe abuse feel that everything was beautiful? This "idealizing the past" process seems counterintuitive and mysterious, but it has a straightforward explanation. As children, we are deeply dependent on our primary caretakers. If we're being seriously hurt by them, we have no choice but to recast the situation in a more positive light, so that we can maintain some feeling of connection with them. This is vitally important to our sense of safety.

People who have grown up in a family in which they were hurt by a parent's abuse or betrayal or enmeshment must reshape the way they view these experiences by "forgetting" the feelings that went with the events. In their left brain they might remember what happened, even while forgetting the feelings that give it significance. Sometimes, however, even the memory of what happened has been forgotten. In either case, the painful or frightening feelings have been disconnected from the memories, and these feelings are stored in the unconscious and attach themselves to other situations or people.

For example, one of my clients, when he was five years old, witnessed his father having an affair. He saw his father flirting and being seductive with a woman. There was sexually suggestive language and excessive touching. My client did not see them having sexual intercourse, but he knew that something was wrong. By the time he was consulting with me, he had forgotten about it, but he had intense reactions to people having affairs. On a slight provocation, he got very moralistic, condemning, and shaming, more than most people. He'd forgotten the event, but he remembered the feelings.

This is typical. The feelings associated with traumatic (painful or frightening) events have not been lost. They are preserved in the right brain. They come out at times of stress, often being projected onto others—for example, onto a woman who is "pressuring" a MEM for commitment. Observing these projected feelings in moments of stress is one of the main ways that they are made visible for analysis. See the next box.

It is common to project feelings associated with one's mother or father onto partners. A client will tell me: "My mother had affairs on my father, and so I couldn't trust my mother. Now I just can't make myself trust my wife, even though she is faithful and there's no reason for me to mistrust her." He's projecting his feelings of mistrust onto his wife, even though they belong to his mother.

PROJECTING FEELINGS

When a person's unconscious is provoked under stress to generate feelings from the past, the person often associates those feelings with someone in the present, thereby "projecting" the feelings onto someone at hand rather than someone from long ago. A MEM's relationships are affected by this projecting of feelings, because he often feels the pain of childhood enmeshment when he is with his partner.

Early Attachment Determines What
Kind of Lover You Will Be

Psychologists refer to the early experiences of a child connecting with his mother (and significant others) as "early attachment." The memory of early attachment is wired in the right brain as an unconscious template by which the child, and the adult the child becomes, experiences other intimate relationships. If early attachment goes well, then this relationship of the child with the mother becomes a gateway to fulfilling, loving, and joyful adult love experiences. Early attachment going well means:

- The baby is given adequate attention, comfort, and stability through consistent, loving caretaking.
- Following the initial stage of infancy, the toddler is given the freedom to be separate from the mother, to explore the world and then return to her as his "secure base."
- A stressful occurrence is usually followed by a reconnection with the mother and soothing by her.

Every child needs a balance between bonding and separation in early childhood. The freedom to come and go is essential to healthy development, and it serves a critical element in being able to merge and separate from a lover in adulthood.

If early attachment does not go well, then the resulting stunted early mother-child relationship serves as the gateway to disappointment and lack of fulfillment in adult love relationships. Early attachment can go badly if there is some form of severe neglect or abuse, so that the baby does not feel safe, or if the toddler's path to separateness is disrupted, as in the case of mother-son enmeshment.

In mother-son enmeshment, the mother inverts the parent-child relationship, so that the boy is now being used to stabilize the needy mother rather than the other way around. The child's adoring attention soothes the inner emotional storms of the mother's feelings; it calms her anxious, fearful, and angry moods. But then his natural need for autonomy arises, beginning at the age of two or three and then at later times throughout childhood. (Many people assume the need for autonomy begins in adolescence, but this isn't true.) He wants to feel free to come and go without negative consequences; he needs to avoid the burden of having to placate his mother's disappointment. But the enmeshing mother feels threatened when her adoring, loving, reassuring son now is poised to withdraw her source of emotional well-being. She feels that his departure—as natural as it is—is dangerous to her happiness and emotional stability. Unconsciously, and sometimes consciously, she begins to bind him to her. She has the power to be successful in enmeshing him, but this happens at a huge cost to the son's future happiness.

Narcissistic Parenting

Very young children need to feel special and valuable in the adoring attention of their mothers and fathers. Children feel this way when their parents are attuned to them and respond to their cues: picking them up when they cry and letting them go when they want to squirm away. In narcissistic parenting, the children can get attention, but the attention serves the needs of the parents rather than the children. The children are picked up when the parents need an emotional boost. They are ignored when the parents have something else to do. Narcissistically parented children grow into adults with an emptiness in their hearts and a sense of bottomless need.

The damage of narcissistic parenting gets passed down the generations. Not only does a child who was narcissistically parented carry the resulting emptiness and need into adulthood, but also, when that adult becomes a parent, the emptiness and need gets expressed as his or her own narcissistic parenting, and so on.

Narcissistic parenting can vary in severity. A mother can be somewhat attuned to her son, but lose her sense of attunement because she is stressed by an absent husband or economic difficulties or lack of resources of some other kind. Under stress, her right brain overrides her good mothering decisions, and she starts to depend on her son to soothe her anxious feelings. However, in the most severe form of narcissistic mothering, the enmeshment is not just the right brain acting under stress.

In the extreme, an enmeshing mother may consciously feel entitled to use her son to fill up her own emptiness, and she may be desperate to keep his loving attention for herself alone. If her husband raises the issue of enmeshment with her, suggesting she become aware of her tendencies and perhaps join him in counseling, this consciously enmeshing mother becomes antagonistic rather than cooperative. She feels that she cannot live without her son's constant adoration, and she doesn't want to talk about it.

Early attachment experiences are imprinted in the right brain in the first years of life, and they are reactivated in adulthood, becoming feelings and sensations during intimate encounters. If all goes well with early attachment, the brain will "remember" feelings of safety and security. If enmeshment occurs, danger and anxiety will be the emotional charge projected into the adult encounter, regardless of whether the adult situation is unsafe or not. This is why it is unreasonable to say to a MEM, "Why don't you just leave your mother? I don't see why it's such a big problem." Or, "Just commit to your girlfriend. She's good for you." His problem is wired in his brain; it's not something he can just will away.

How to "Fix" the Past

A fundamental approach of psychotherapy is to retrieve from the unconscious the feelings that give significance to traumatic childhood events and to help the MEM to reassociate these feelings with their memories. A goal of psychotherapy is to learn to process intrusions of the unconscious at moments of stress and to avoid repeating mistakes driven by unconscious templates.

Here is a story from my client, Larry, after he had learned to recognize and modify his unconscious reactions. "I screamed at my kid over nothing. I couldn't believe it. It reminded me of my mother screaming at me. It took me back. I cried, and I told a good friend about it. And you know what? I'm not going to do that again."

Here is what Larry did:

1. He understood that he was out of line.
2. He recognized the unconscious roots of his behavior, what it related to in his childhood and how he was triggered.
3. He felt the strong feelings from the past that drove his behavior.
4. He expressed points 1 to 3 clearly to someone else, in the spirit of clarity, humility, and accountability.

5. He used the clarity of points 1 to 4 to resolve to change his behavior.

Larry recognized an intrusion of his unconscious at a moment of stress in his life, and he dealt with it for what it was.

Everyone gets provoked into unconscious templates, and when this happens, most people ignore or minimize it. Larry understood what had happened and took himself through the process, because I had taught him how to do it in therapy. Many people don't have the humility or the patience to find their way through all these steps. Even more fundamental, most people don't have the willingness. Sometimes therapy is about teaching clients to be willing to consider a different way to view themselves.

In the next chapter, I give some further information about how this process works in therapy.

10 THE HEALING JOURNEY
About Therapy

The purpose of psychotherapy is to uncover the workings of the unconscious mind in order to gain control over destructive behaviors, troublesome moods, or barriers to a more fulfilled and happy life. Therapy is not offering advice to people about their personal problems. It is not coaching. It is a kind of archeological excavation to dig up old unconscious patterns and reactions. It is uncomfortable. It takes time. It requires expert guidance. This chapter's purpose is to help you understand what therapy is, when it is needed, what should happen in therapy, and how to choose a therapist.

Psychotherapy Is Not Sympathetic Listening
You might be wondering what the difference is between psychotherapy and other modes of emotional problem solving—for example, sympathetic listening, positive thinking, willpower, "just say no," and a legion of others. Why should you pay a therapist, when your priest or a good friend will listen and offer guidance for free? The difference is the way psychotherapy works to access the unconscious basis of behavior. Sympathetic listening is a supportive process: When you present a problem,

emotional support and encouragement are offered, often along with advice on ways to deal with the problem. This kind of support is often helpful. However, it is *not* therapy. Today many people are getting "life coaching" to help them through personal or business problems. This also is not therapy. Life coaching essentially addresses only the conscious mind.

Usually, when people get into serious emotional or behavioral problems that they want to change but "can't," their unconscious templates are controlling them. Psychotherapists know this and are trained to work to uncover these unconscious root causes and help people be less influenced by them. A priest, minister, rabbi, or other morals-based counselor generally will be dealing only with conscious material. He or she may suggest "forgiveness" as a way to change. However, the unconscious obeys its own rules. A person, acting according to moral principles, can suppress certain behaviors and impulses that have unconscious roots, but then the unconscious energy will emerge in some other way. For example, a MEM might suppress his rage at his mother. Then his unconscious might emerge to express that rage by womanizing and simultaneously damning other men's sexual behavior.

FORGIVENESS

Forgiving is important to spiritual growth and healing. However, some people use forgiveness to deny rather than to reconcile problems and feelings. When this happens, the unconscious still has its way, and the problems persist. Forgiveness without facing these problems and feelings is just another form of denial.

♺

People who want to change their behavior patterns need to deal with the stories embedded in their unconscious minds. Only then can their morality be synchronized with their behavior. That's where psychotherapy comes in. It is the only process which does that job.

What Causes Depression?

A MEM is not going to be coming in my door saying he had a rotten family and a bad childhood. Often he will focus on his depression and ask me to help him get some medication to combat it. However, it wouldn't make sense just to recommend antidepressant drugs and send him away. If he's going to get better, it is important to find out why he's depressed.

Depression sometimes can result from a biological issue—and therefore be properly treated by drugs—but that diagnosis is often overused. Depression also can be caused by an undifferentiated mass of feelings that has never been processed. If that mass of frozen feelings is thawed, pretty soon the MEM isn't so depressed anymore. And even more important, he has become more aligned with his True Self. A MEM has a core story that his unconscious is desperate to tell. When this storytelling process is allowed to happen, the MEM is then more free to be himself. He is less controlled by his unconscious templates.

Do You Need Therapy?

"Are you a MEM?" is best answered by considering the questionnaire at the beginning of Chapter 9. The following list focuses more specifically on the issue of whether you need therapy. As noted in Chapter 9, the seriousness of the consequences of mother-son enmeshment varies for different MEM. Not all MEM need therapy. On the other hand, a MEM who does need therapy will not get enough help merely by reading this (or any other) book or by finding a friend or religious advisor to talk to.

If you recognize these points as pertaining to you, then consider therapy:

- *Minimizing.* You have a destructive habit, and you know there is a problem, but you minimize it. You say, "This isn't a big deal," or, "This is a problem, but I can handle it myself." But you never do handle it. We could be talking here about difficulties with relationships, commitment, sexual problems, eating too much or drinking too much, working too much, or having no get-up-and-go.

- *Avoiding.* Some aspect of your behavior bothers you, but you don't want to think about it. You may be "in denial." See the box titled "Denial" in Chapter 7.

- *Can't change.* Some aspect of your behavior or your life bothers you, and you've tried to make things better, but you haven't succeeded. Your conscious will alone isn't up to the job.

- *Troubled sexuality.* Some aspect of your sexuality bothers you. You may have difficulty with performance, or your sexuality may be suppressed, or it may be excessive, compulsive, or disturbing in some other way.

- *Feeling anxious or depressed.* Anxiety or depression is limiting your life.

- *Can't say no.* You cannot set limits with people—such as your mother or your partner—who make unreasonable demands on your time and energy.

- *Betrayal bond*. You have a relationship as described in Chapter 8 as a betrayal bond. For example, you may have misplaced loyalty, in the sense that you are loyal to people, situations, relationships, or institutions that are hurtful or harmful to you.

Barriers to Therapy for a MEM

A MEM may need therapy, and he may admit he needs therapy, and then—to the frustration of the people who love him—he may avoid therapy. One common pattern is for him to dabble in therapy without taking it seriously, perhaps by changing therapists often or not going to therapy for long periods.

A MEM has some built-in barriers to therapy that deter him. The primary barrier is the Disloyalty Bind; in other words, his guilt about being disloyal to Mom by making his own life choices. He also commonly is afraid that he will hurt Mom just by talking about her. He will tend to cling to the idealized and sanitized story of his childhood: He was Mom's hero, and he suffered no damage. She was perfect and a martyr.

When he begins to be aware of all the losses of his enmeshment-stunted life, he may become very angry. His fear of that anger may become in itself an obstacle to self-knowledge. Of course, he may have difficulty linking his current behaviors to his history and his unconscious templates. He certainly will have difficulty setting boundaries with Mom and other people, which is something therapy will lead to. The biggest barrier to his pursuing therapy may be the challenge to make a definite decision to reclaim his life.

What Should Happen in Therapy, and What Is the Therapeutic Time Line?

If therapy goes according to plan, you can transform your life in two to five years of once-a-week sessions. Less than two years is possible but not common.

In the first year of therapy, your focus will be on clarifying what you are dealing with. You must address and learn to manage any addictions before you can make further progress. As you move into the second year, you continue to recognize, acknowledge, and clarify the losses in your life. You will also begin to develop some new behaviors and make some changes—for example, you'll be able to tell Mom, "Sometimes I can't return your call until the next day." In your second year of therapy, you are finding your authentic self. You've had many "roles" imposed on you, as described in Chapter 8. Now you begin to find alternatives and choices, using the boundaries that you now know how to implement. You are reworking the Disloyalty Bind and confronting toxic guilt and other false beliefs.

From your third year of therapy until you are done, you will practice your new, healthier behaviors. There are people in your life who aren't helping you. Either those relationships must change to something more positive, or you must let them go. You can continue to have a relationship with your mother, but you cannot stay "married to Mom."

After therapy, you live your new life. You have a new set of values. You have a new commitment to have a family, a new career, or other improvements. You have a new set of relationships that validate the new you. For difficult relationships that you have decided to maintain, you have clear boundaries that make them safe and workable. Your life is now its own healing agent, and the healing is self-sustaining. You might need to return to therapy if you relapse into your addictions or if you find yourself struggling with some of your original difficulties. Otherwise, enjoy your hard-earned good life.

NECESSARY ELEMENTS OF SUCCESSFUL PSYCHOTHERAPY

- Recovering from addictions
- Making the unconscious conscious
- Clarifying family-of-origin and enmeshment issues
- Reshaping emotional responses and relationships
- Learning to have boundaries
- Forgiving and letting go

Marshaling Resources

Self-neglect is one of the symptoms of a MEM, yet it is critical that he find in himself the will to get better. Arthur from Chapter 8 is stuck in a bad job that is getting worse, because his Disloyalty Bind won't let him leave. He cannot find in himself the inner resources to enable him to reach out for help. He says, "Yes, you're right. I should take action, but I can't." These are the words of a man who has been exhausted by his unconscious struggle.

In contrast, a recovering MEM will have found the will to travel the healing journey. Although "willpower" alone won't cure him, persistence and commitment are important, because he has to do things that don't "feel good." His right brain is acting to saturate his steps to freedom with guilt and fear. His left brain has to be able to move him along until his right brain can be taught new patterns.

Commitment is the steadfast left brain keeping to the path in spite of the troublesome feelings the right brain is generating. When it comes time for MEM to exercise commitment in the service of making their lives better, the unconscious floods their emotions with the old feelings of engulfment. They then resist and rebel against the thing that is stimulating these bad feelings, namely, commitment. In particular, the process of therapy itself can cause this response and therefore evoke resistance. You may recall that this resistance came up in therapy for Doug (Chapter 2).

I have to be careful as a therapist not to give too much advice. At first, a MEM client is eager to please and wants suggestions, but over time, he begins to experience my advice as controlling. He transfers feelings to his therapy experience that he felt in his enmeshment experience. Instead, I work to empower him. "What do you think are some ways to handle the issue?" I might say. "Of these suggestions what 'feels right' to you?" In this way, I am aligning with his True Self, the part of him that wants to be free and in charge. If I give too much advice, his False Self may be induced to pretend to agree while offering passive resistance, its natural response to feeling controlled.

A MEM is often confused about where he wants to go with his life and how to get help. In fact, he often resists knowing this. He tends to think in terms of finding someone to turn his life over to. He may look to his therapist, his priest, or his new woman to tell him what to do. This thinking reflects the MEM's enmeshment issues. To find freedom, a MEM needs to learn to take responsibility for his own healing.

How Do You Choose a Therapist?

Finding and approaching a therapist can seem like a difficult chore, but I'll try to make it easier here. Let's try looking at choosing a therapist as a series of steps, each of which has a specific focus.

Before Contacting a Therapist

Not all therapists will be equally good for you. Try to get references from friends or, if you attend a support group such as Alcoholics Anonymous, the people in your support group. Look for a therapist who understands enmeshment. Relevant specialties are men's issues, childhood abuse, sexual abuse, and addictions. Avoid a therapist with a reputation for endless therapy with little results, and also avoid anyone committed to very short-term therapy. When therapists suggest short-term therapy to deal with enmeshment issues, they often are hampered by insurance constraints or may not fully understand the implications of enmeshment. See the following box.

Telephone Call

Most therapists will be willing to talk with you briefly before you commit to a session with them. Say what issues you think you have: minimizing, avoiding, can't change, troubled sexuality, and so on. Say you think you are enmeshed with your mother. Ask if the therapist has treated other people with your issues. If not, ask if this therapist can refer you to another therapist who has. Ask about the therapist's approach and determine if the answer seems clear and reasonable. Ask what the therapist charges and about possible insurance coverage.

First Session

Tell the therapist you are overinvolved with your mother. The fundamental question you need to have the therapist answer is

SHORT-TERM THERAPY AND MANAGED CARE

What it is. *Short-term therapy limits the time the
therapist and client have together, sometimes to no more
than twelve sessions, regardless of the client's actual needs.
"Managed care" refers to limiting the funds for therapy
to save the insurance company money.*
Why it doesn't lead to lasting changes. *When therapy is
artificially time-limited, successful long-term changes in
behavior are unlikely. Short-term therapy focuses on symptom
management. For example, a depressed person might be given
antidepressant medication without psychotherapy. Research
strongly suggests that the combination of both is most effective.*
What it leads to. *A therapist trying to help clients under
managed care often gives up trying to uncover root causes.
The therapy process may be reduced to "coaching."*

✑

"Have you worked with adults to help them de-enmesh and differentiate from their parents in order to begin to lead successful
lives?" Although you asked about this in the telephone call, it is
an important issue, and you need to be very clear about it. If the
therapist appears not to have this kind of hands-on experience
with enmeshment issues, ask for a colleague who has. If the
therapist has had this kind of experience, ask for specific success
stories. Make sure the therapist doesn't minimize your issue. If a
therapist seems detached, or distracted, or not paying attention,
or "off" in some other way, trust your intuition and look elsewhere. A therapist needs to suit you at a deep intuitive level.

Over the First Six Sessions

You should feel listened to. The therapist should establish rapport and trust with you. If you don't have a sense of being understood and validated within six sessions, change therapists.

In his or her feedback, the therapist should show that he or she grasps your problem. Also, the therapist should be neither overly pushy nor minimizing. It's a bad sign if the therapist's immediate reaction is "Gee, this sounds really bad. You should cut off your relationship with your mother." On the other hand, the therapist who says "What's the big deal about being too close to your mother?" probably isn't going to be able to work effectively with you on these issues.

Ask the therapist what he or she thinks are the problems associated with parent-child enmeshment. Note that MEM tend to want the therapist to say it's not a problem. Enmeshment is scary to confront, and the most comforting feedback from a therapist would be "You don't have to deal with it." However, this response indicates that the therapist will *not* be helpful.

Before, During, and After Therapy but Not Instead of Therapy

A troubled MEM can pursue three activities, besides therapy, to improve his life. First, he can attend a support group at least once a week. If the MEM suspects that he might have an unhealthy relationship to an addictive substance or process (alcohol, drugs, food, spending, codependency, sex), he might want to attend a twelve-step group that focuses on his addiction. (Twelve-step groups are based on Alcoholics Anonymous, and people with addictions often find them helpful.) If he doesn't have a problem of this sort, he might attend a support group that addresses his excessive "caretaking" (perhaps

Codependents Anonymous). I list contact information for a range of support groups at the end of this book. Attending a support group offers the basic benefit of creating fellowship, which is very healing for MEM.

Second, a MEM should read about recovery: dysfunctional families, enmeshment, addictions, child abuse, depression, whatever he intuitively thinks might be helpful. Reading this book is a very good start. I know it can be difficult to look at MEM issues, and you should feel proud that you are doing it. Workbooks are especially useful. Reading and workbooking should be combined with journaling, which is simply keeping a running set of notes in a personal recovery journey. When a MEM has a strong emotional reaction to something he reads (fear, disgust, excitement, shame), then what he is reading may reflect his unconscious story, even if he does not recognize or remember anything in his life that it is related to. He should note these passages in the journal. They are important.

Since it can be difficult to "get started" journaling, here are some ideas that my MEM clients have found helpful. Write the story of your childhood as you would have wanted it to be: what would it have been like, if you had not been enmeshed? Another exercise is to list your heart's true desires, both as a child and now as an adult, things you might have been prevented from doing because of your enmeshment. Are these the things that you would like to be doing now? Try to imagine (and write down): If you didn't feel guilty and obligated today, how would your life be and what would you be doing differently? How would the next five years go? My final suggestion for journaling is to list the kinds of relationships that you desire, both romances and friendships.

The last of the three activities that I recommend is actually something to avoid: limit damaging relationships. To the extent that he can, a MEM should limit unpleasant or hurtful interactions with people. A MEM often feels obligated to get together with people, say family members, when he doesn't want to. He should note his feelings about such personal encounters in his journal.

These three activities will move a MEM *toward* consciousness, fellowship, and taking responsibility and *away from* addictions and unhealthy habits and relationships. They are powerful healing steps, even though they are not substitutes for therapy.

Moving Forward

The fundamental purpose of psychotherapy is to reduce the power of a MEM's unconscious templates to control his life. Barriers to therapy come up in confronting the guilt and denial generated by enmeshment. The need to remember how bad things felt as a child is one of the main challenges to success in therapy for anyone, but especially for MEM.

Having considered the goals and methods of healing in Part Two, we now put our focus in Part Three on relationships.

PART THREE

❧

How Do You Build Healthy Relationships?

11 BEING YOUR OWN MAN

How a MEM Can Make Things Better with Parents, Siblings, and Others

The healing journey for a MEM includes trying to develop his relationship with his father and limit his relationship with his mother. At first, the idea of negotiating with his mother can seem terrifying and with his father impossible, but this chapter offers techniques for accomplishing it.

Fundamental to making things better with both parents is the idea of *boundaries*. A MEM can learn to make his own voice heard in his connections with his parents by explicitly setting limits and rules to change the old ways he related to them. I know it sounds paradoxical, but building healthy relationships really does require setting boundaries and limits. These kinds of limits allow people to maintain a sense of themselves while connecting with others; the alternatives are to be engulfed or distant. Because of their long history of enmeshment, MEM find it difficult to negotiate the middle ground in relationships. They expect to be merged with a person or distant from him or her.

A MEM had his boundaries ignored and intruded on when he was a child, at a time when his ability to say no was developing. Now, as an adult, he struggles to have boundaries, and he has trouble saying no. There is great power in being explicit about what is acceptable and what is not. If a MEM remains firm in his reasonable requests to his parents, they may acquiesce. If not, at least he is more clear on who he is and what he wants, an achievement in itself.

Healthy Mother-Son Closeness

Before continuing, perhaps we should consider what healthy mother-son relationships look like, in contrast with enmeshed relationships. A man who is close to, but not enmeshed with, his mother has his own set of values and his own sense of self distinct from his mother's. His contact with his mother may be regular, because he loves her and they're connected by a lifetime of shared experiences. However, his relationship with his mother is not the main one in his life; his relationships with himself and his wife and children come first. Also, his mother's relationship with him is not primary for her either. She has her own interests and relationships independent of him.

A nonenmeshed son's contact with his mother does not have the sense of weary obligation that it often does for MEM. Also, the nonenmeshing mother is respectful of her son's separateness; for example, the mother doesn't burden her son with her personal problems, and the son doesn't feel compelled to rescue his mother when she has personal problems. There may be periods in which he is involved with his mother's concerns, but not chronically. He knows he is not his mother's primary support.

The Bottom Line

A successful relationship will have a "bottom line" for both people. This is the understanding that there are limits to what will be endured. It is not a threat but an explicit establishing of boundaries: "I'll do everything I can to make this work with you, but in the end, if you hurt me, if you exploit me, if you betray me, if you neglect me and do nothing about it, I will not stay with you. If this relationship is only about your needs and you make no effort to make it about me, in spite of my pleas, I have the right to say good-bye. I will leave you, if I have to." In healthy relationships, this bottom line is often unspoken but understood. However, when there is trouble in a relationship, it is a good move to be clear about your bottom line.

MEM need this kind of clarity not just with their parents, but with siblings, partners, children, friends—everyone that a MEM wants a close relationship with. MEM find the concept of the bottom line difficult, because they are terrified of displeasing or allowing give-and-take in a relationship. They fear retaliation. They fear rejection. They fear abandonment. They fear the other person will "take over."

Every MEM discussed in this book had difficulty setting a reasonable bottom line in his relationships. Father Mark from Chapter 4 needed to learn how; his limitless devotion to his calling and his food addiction would have killed him, had he not finally found his bottom line. Freddy set limits on Angela's affairs (Chapter 7). The marriage ended, but Freddy was able to restart his life. Tony had a bottom line imposed by Elizabeth, which eventually was good for him (Chapter 3).

John and Linda Friel put it this way in their book *The 7 Best Things Happy Couples Do:* "Really great couples are willing to end it all, and so they never have to." What the Friels are expressing here is that by having clear limits that could lead to divorce, each person in the couple affirms commitment to a healthy, clarified relationship. Otherwise, the power difference between them will make one of them "disappear," and the relationship will eventually be empty for both. The Friels' book focuses on romantic connections, but the principle of the bottom line applies to other close relationships too.

Setting Boundaries with Mom

Before he can set boundaries with his mother, a MEM needs to be clear with himself that his relationship with her was—and still is—excessive, burdensome, and inappropriate. His guilt is not a good measure of reality. His response is out of proportion with her true need and his true obligation to her.

Here is a step-by-step process for a MEM to set boundaries with his mother:

Step 1. Make a list of the ten most burdensome, inappropriate caretaking things you do for your mother, ordered from the most damaging and difficult to the least. For example, suppose she habitually asks you to come over on Saturday night—when you want to go out with your fiancée—because she's lonely and she's worried about burglars. So you wind up going over there frequently on Saturday nights. That might be "number one" on your list. Number ten might be her daily phone call to you at work. "It's just me," she says, expecting to chat for half an hour.

Step 2. Write down a few statements that are clear and specific ways of setting limits, such as, "No. I am unable to do that for you," or, "I can't talk now. I will call you tomorrow." You should practice these statements out loud, so that you don't change your position under the stress of talking to her. These statements represent your boundaries. One effective way to practice is to pretend your mother is in the room with you or on the phone. Imagine her asking you to do something on your list.

Then say to her, "No. I am not available to help you with that," or whatever statements you have written down.

Step 3. Identify the feelings that come up as you practice your "boundary statements" and talk about them with someone. Ideally, you will get support from your therapist or a good friend or someone else who is supportive of you and understands your enmeshment issues. Typically you will feel an emotional hangover of disloyalty, guilt, and fear of retaliation. Therapy will help you process these uncomfortable feelings and lessen the inappropriate guilt.

Step 4. List the things that your mother does that trigger your guilt or fear the most. Does she get weepy? Does she become a martyr? Does she show disappointment? Does she show anger? Does she get silent? Does she threaten retaliation? You need to anticipate your reactions to these triggers, then write them down and think about them. In this way, you will prepare yourself. When she says, "Oh, God, no one loves me anymore," you will be ready with a truthful reply that reaffirms your boundaries.

Step 5. Work to develop a set of new beliefs to counter the false beliefs that you learned as a child. See the next box. These new beliefs can function as affirmations to support your efforts to set boundaries with Mom.

NEW BELIEFS FOR MEM

1. It was not my responsibility, when I was a little boy, to take care of my mother. It is not my responsibility today.

2. It is okay to have my own life and be separate from my mother.

3. It is okay to need what I need, want what I want, and desire what I desire. I can pursue my needs, wants, and desires, as long as I behave responsibly.

4. It is okay to feel and express my passion in all areas of my life, including sexual passion. My passion is mine, not my mother's.

5. I am responsible for my sexual expression. It is there for me to enjoy, not to suppress or act out.

6. I am not being disloyal to my mother when I have a satisfying relationship with a woman.

7. Fantasy will not bring me intimacy.

8. There is no perfect partner. I deserve to have a realistic relationship with someone I desire.

9. I do not have to stay in any relationship I don't want. It's okay to leave a relationship and look for a partner I like.

10. In relationships, I am not being entrapped or engulfed. That is a memory. I have the choice to set boundaries, to take time to consider what I want, or to end a relationship.

11. It is okay to be intimate at my own pace.

12. Commitment means the *choice* to stay, not the *demand* to be loyal no matter what happens.

How to Be with Mom

Learning to set boundaries is important for a MEM to enable him to have a healthy relationship with his mother, but exactly what kind of relationship should he want to have with her? Does he take her shopping? If so, when and for how long? Does he limit what they talk about to avoid conflicts? Making these kinds of clear and specific decisions around Mom is a dilemma for a MEM because of his fear, guilt, shame, and low self-esteem. Also, as parents age, there is a natural tendency to want to care for them. This complicates the dilemma of a MEM trying to be emotionally separate.

A MEM who is constantly on call needs to work out a new arrangement with his mom. One option is to offer Saturday afternoon (or some other specific time) to help her with chores at the house for a fixed number of hours. This would be a way for him to give his mother some special time without having it control his life, because it is scheduled and limited in scope. Some of my MEM clients have boundaries on physical contact—for example, a hug "hello" but not a kiss. Things like this can be important to a recovering MEM, who is newly aware that his mother is often uncomfortably close.

Aside from ground rules for *getting together* and *physical touch,* the typical boundaries my MEM clients want to set with their mothers are on *topics of conversation* and *money.* A MEM might ask his mother not to talk about his father (or his girlfriend or his wife), if his mother tends to vent and triangulate her son with their disagreements. I discuss this further below, in the section about parents together.

Money can raise enormous enmeshment issues, whether Mom is giving money to him or he is giving money to her. Mom may be giving her MEM money, or he might be waiting for an inheritance from her. Either of these situations can become a way for her to control him and keep him enmeshed. I've seen many MEM disabled by being financially dependent on their mothers. A MEM has to be willing to set boundaries with Mom, as discussed. If he won't act for fear of losing the money, he will never become his own man.

What about the reverse situation, where the MEM's mother is always asking him for money, or she is chronically in financial difficulty and he feels obligated to give her money? The way it often happens is that the MEM will get phone calls from his sister or his brother: "Mom needs some money. She doesn't want to ask you. I'm asking you for her." What should he do, particularly if the requests are chronic? His difficulty may be either that he can't spare the money or that giving the money puts him in the emotional bind that he's struggling to free himself from.

He needs to make some definite decisions. What are his rules around money going to be? And keeping these boundaries, like all boundaries with Mom, may require the full program of preparation described earlier. He could decide that he's not available to give money, particularly if looks like she can do okay without it. Another option is to give only for a legitimate emergency. One client of mine will give his mother money only when it advances her independence. When she was fighting the government to get her Social Security—she was completely disabled and officials were giving her a hard time—he said, "Let's get a lawyer, I'll pay for it." The lawyer took her through the process and made sure she would get her benefits. The son was happy to pay, because he knew it would help her be more independent.

How to Connect with Dad

A MEM needs to start having a relationship with his father independent of his mother. He should do this if his parents are still together, or if they are divorced, or even if his father is deceased. The MEM can have a relationship with his father at some level. The idea is to *have his own version of his father* rather than his mother's version. The son may still decide he doesn't like his father. Let that be the son's independent decision, based on his own perceptions. If his father is deceased, the MEM can write him a letter, visit his grave, or talk about him with some of his old friends. He can express his love, loss, or anger, or all three. He shouldn't be surprised if he feels that he is going to be punished for violating his mother's point of view.

Assuming that Dad's alive and available, a MEM should try to spend time with him without his mother. At the same time, old destructive patterns should be avoided. Father Mark's father was an alcoholic. He'd go to the corner bar and stay there, abandoning his son. When Father Mark first came to see me, his idea of connecting with his father was to take the train to Chicago and go sit with him on a barstool and drink. He relished and romanticized these encounters, as he had concluded that this was the best he could get.

But this kind of connecting is not what I'm suggesting. Father Mark in the bar with his father was acting out some of the most painful parts of his childhood. Because I didn't think joining his father this way was really helping him, I advised him to find a different activity. Sometimes Father Mark did manage to get his father to join him at restaurants that didn't serve alcohol.

When a MEM decides to have adult relationships with dysfunctional parents, he cannot avoid some additional losses. He's been doing things "their way" his whole life. Now he has to decide between the losses associated with his compromises and the losses that result from being true to himself.

That's really the issue here. If the father can't have a relationship with his son *based to some extent on the son's needs,* then that's a loss the son is going to have to live with. The loss can be in one of three forms, but with a similar impact. First, if the son continues to keep company with his father, when the father won't change a thing for him, then the son will feel the abandonment of his father's indifference. Second, if the son breaks with his father then he will still feel abandoned, along with the physical abandonment. In my experience, most fathers will be agreeable to change, except those who are severely alcoholic, addicted, narcissistic, or sociopathic. Even some of the more insensitive fathers will respond, particularly later in life.

NARCISSISTS

Narcissists have a persistent pattern of relating to the world as if everyone is an extension of their own wishes. Expressing your needs to a narcissist is not the experience of "being ignored." It is the experience of "being unrecognized." There is a difference. Being ignored means he knows you're there, but he's not paying attention to you. With a narcissist, you're not there as a separate person at all. That is, you're there on his radar screen, but only as an extension of himself. You're not being seen as who you are: someone who is separate and who might have separate needs.

The third form of loss is the most common: The father may be agreeable, but he simply doesn't have much to share with his son. Realizing that he doesn't can be devastating to a son's fantasy of eventual love and reconciliation. Whatever he gets now from his father is going to be much less than he wanted as a child. It may be very painful to see how little his father has to offer.

There are similar losses, of course, when a MEM sets boundaries with his mother. If he says, "I can't have you always complaining about Dad to me," she may not be able to stop, she may not be willing to stop, or she may have no interest in stopping. Then he has to decide how much he is willing to participate in this relationship under those conditions. It will cost him something if he stays around and something if he leaves. Under both scenarios, he is being subjected to a form of abandonment.

Further, the MEM is going to have to give up his special status as "mom's little man." He has always compensated for his Disloyalty Bind with his sense that he is important to Mom. This fantasy will fade as he begins to normalize his relationship with his mother, and then he will need to develop new ways to feel good about himself.

I have a client now, Mathew, who is a fairly well-known entertainer. His father is an actor, and he is very narcissistic. He hadn't seen his son for twenty years, but finally he came to visit. Narcissists love to argue, and the father attempted to bait his son by saying some outrageous things about his mother. Mathew decided that he wasn't going to let his father control the conversation that way. He decided to change the way he had habitually responded by not arguing. His father continued to criticize and provoke, and Mathew wouldn't go there with him. Pretty soon his father stopped trying to start a fight and settled down to a rather mild visit.

The next time I saw him, Mathew said, "Gee, my father's different."

I said, "No. Your father's not different. You're different. Your father just had a new response, because you're operating with a new set of rules. You're not reacting. You're not taking things personally. You're not giving him ammunition."

If Mathew had chosen to engage with his father in the old way, he would have been emotionally hung over and depressed. No doubt he would have been telling me that he had acted out sexually, which was his way of releasing emotional tension. Instead, he felt quite good. Mathew had a new set of rules for his *own* behavior, independent of what his father chose to do. In this case, his father responded positively, but that isn't always the case.

A narcissistic father won't be able to "hear" that his son has made a request. The son says, "I don't want to go to a place where they serve alcohol," and his father responds with, "Let's go to . . ." and names his favorite place to drink. There's no recognition of his son or his son's request. If his son replies, "I'm not going to that restaurant with you," his father might go alone.

Mothers can be narcissistic too. You might say to a narcissistic mother, "I don't want to talk about Father," and a few minutes later she's talking about him. She doesn't recognize your needs as separate from hers. She wants to talk about your father, so that must be okay with you too. I always recommend two books to clients with narcissistic parents: *The Wizard of Oz and Other Narcissists* by Eleanor Payson and *Children of the Self-Absorbed* by Nina W. Brown.

I worked with a client, Tom, who wanted his narcissistic father to show him some love and acknowledgment. It was a difficult struggle. Tom would call his parents, and his dad would answer the call.

"This is Tom."

"Here's your mother," his dad would say, passing the phone away.

Then Tom learned to say "I don't want to talk to Mom. I

want to talk to you." Of course, after only about thirty seconds, he'd get "Here's your mother."

Finally Tom could manage "I don't want to talk to Mother. I want to talk to you. I called to talk to you." This was a very difficult boundary for Tom to set. Even so, his father never had much to say to him.

Tom was scared, and this fear made progress difficult. He was having to face the question: *Could his father respond to him?* After each encounter, he would feel the weakness of his father's response. He was having to let go of his fantasy that his father could one day take delight in him, the way Tom had wanted as a little boy. It was too late. Since his father was a narcissist, it had always been too late.

How to Deal with Mom and Dad Together

As an adult, the MEM may find himself caught up in the same dynamic between his parents that he experienced as a child. For example, suppose he goes to visit, and his mom complains to him about his father in front of the father, as if he is not in the room. Once again she is using her son to get at her husband. She formulates an alliance of two against one, and his father, resenting it, dismisses and rejects his son in response—just as had happened when he was a boy.

This kind of pattern of behavior can be very entrenched. In one case, my client's mother was still complaining to him about his dad and working to draw her son in as her ally, conspirator, and partner against his father—even though his father had died years before.

If a MEM is faced with these old family situations, he has some decisions to make. If he falls back into his old role with his parents, he will pay an emotional price. When he leaves and returns to his own home, he will carry back with him feelings of powerlessness and anger. He may project these feelings onto his wife and start a fight with her. Or he may want to dull his pain with some addictive substance or process. Sam from Chapter 5 turned to alcohol and cybersex after his weekly phone call with his mother.

A MEM shouldn't visit his parents and allow the destructive patterns of behavior from his childhood to continue to occur. At the same time, he may not want to avoid his parents permanently. It's the same as with visiting his parents separately: He has to have some boundaries, and he has to be willing to state them out loud: "It sounds like the two of you are still fighting. I don't want to talk about your difficulties. If you insist on bringing them up with me, I'm leaving."

He can say that to both of them together, or he can say it to each of them individually. But he has to establish a new set of rules for himself, whether his parents agree or not. I would urge him to write them down. Rules might include:

1. I don't respond to my mother's criticisms of my dad.
2. I don't talk to her about my dad.
3. I say out loud to them both that I don't want to talk with either of them about their conflict.

The MEM reads those rules aloud to himself before he goes over to their house. And if he gets into trouble, he goes into the bathroom and rereads them. He comes back out, and he announces them once again to his parents. He at least is honoring his limits, even if his parents are not.

It's important not to hold these boundaries in a way that is too rigid or too loose. People with too-rigid boundaries find it difficult to adapt to change and are unable to let other people into their lives. People with too-loose boundaries have a hard time defining their own agendas and allow people who are hurtful or violating to enter their lives.

SUMMARY OF STEPS FOR SETTING BOUNDARIES

- Recognize there is a problem.
- Define new boundaries—not too rigid, not too loose
- Practice setting the boundaries before actually setting them. Be willing to tolerate the loss, guilt, fear, and shame that may come up when they are set.
- Plan for support after having an encounter around the boundaries.
- Set the boundaries and hold firm.
- Get the support as planned.

As a child, the MEM wanted his parents to respond to him spontaneously. Now he has to carefully structure what he presents to them to get any kind of reasonable response. He grew up fearful and cautious because he couldn't bear the possibility of losing his parents. Finally, as an adult, he's at the point where he can take that risk.

That's when Tom could say to his father, "I don't want to talk to Mother. I want to talk to you." It wasn't much of a conversation, but it was a huge piece of success for Tom. He had claimed something for himself, even if what actually happened wasn't exactly his fantasy. Of course, the next time he called, his father said, "Here's your mother," and the next time he visited, his mother complained about his father. But now Tom knew he could redirect a conversation, if he needed to.

Often a MEM will have to repeat the statement of his boundaries many times, and it's his judgment whether to stop trying to break contact or keep redirecting. But his parents' response is not the point. The recovering MEM will have to let go of his dream of the ideal parents he wanted. As he goes through his healing journey, he may get a little support from them. More important, he has reclaimed his ability to support himself.

Making Things Better with Siblings

A MEM has often played the role of parent to his siblings, but this needs to stop. The first step in making things better is to stop caretaking chronically needy siblings. Often, when he is being "the parent," his siblings view him with contempt and anger. They turn to him inappropriately and make demands on him. And there's really no sibling relationship. When his siblings call him for help and want to vent their woes, he should listen and offer love and support, but he shouldn't offer to fix things. He needs to let go of acting in the role of a parent.

He can say things like "I see you've got a real problem there. I trust that you'll handle it. I have a lot of confidence in you" rather than "Let me come over and help."

That's the difference that he needs to practice, because by going over and helping he is placing himself in the parental role, which is a by-product of his role as a MEM. A MEM often learns to parent his siblings from his mother, because she used him to take over some of her (and his father's) parenting duties.

So, when Mom calls and tells him to go over and take care of Patty, his sister, he needs to learn to tell Mom that he's not going to do it. And he shouldn't allow Patty to call to tell him how much his mother needs him to go over and help her. As he begins to understand these triangulations, he will see how they function to keep him in an unhealthy role. Here again he needs some boundaries. He can list the ways that he is hooked into his sister or brother in a damaging way. Then he can use the same process he used to change his relationship with Mom.

When he's gotten beyond the parent role with his siblings, he will want to try to have social connections with them that don't involve taking care of problems. He could go to a ball game, a movie, a hike, a night at the opera, anything they both enjoy. The key is not to have a problem-solving session.

You might be wondering, "Aren't family members supposed to help family members?" Yes, but we have to consider the long-term patterns: If the need for help by siblings is a repetitive problem that they really should be solving for themselves, what kind of realistic support can or should a brother be offering? Certainly, he will offer affection and encouragement, but he has a right to take care of himself. He is allowed to consider his own needs.

SUMMARY OF HOW TO MAKE THINGS BETTER WITH SIBLINGS

- Do not act out your role as a surrogate parent to your siblings.
- Set boundaries with them if they are excessively needy.
- If they habitually act as agents for your mother or for each other, ask them to stop.
- Develop relationships with them if your connection has been damaged by the enmeshment.

Another kind of dysfunctional relationship arises between a MEM and his siblings. They may be estranged. His siblings may be angry with him, jealous of him, and feel competitive with him, because he was his mother's favorite. His exalted position may have detached him from his siblings. In this case, he may need to show interest and empathy for them and work to develop adult relationships with them.

Beyond Parents and Siblings: Building A Support Network
Many MEM do not have lives distinct from their duties. They tend to be organized around work, their mothers, their siblings, and their other obligatory relationships. MEM are often uncomfortable with social connections, because they feel guilty about having their own interests and they fear getting enmeshed. In fact, MEM do have a tendency to get enmeshed in social relationships, but there are ways of countering that.

It's important to have friendships outside the family. Often a MEM did not develop friends as a child, because they interfered with the "best friendship" of Mom. It follows that many MEM are socially isolated. A MEM should take seriously the need to change this. Even a few hours a week of social contact can make a big difference in his happiness.

One powerful form of fellowship available to MEM is a support group. There is a deep satisfaction in gathering with people who are humbly seeking to make themselves better. Being in a support group can lead to significant acquaintanceships or friendships.

However, a MEM shouldn't limit himself to organizations devoted to problem solving. Social groups provide places where MEM can practice being around people and being connected to people without being enmeshed. MEM can connect with a variety of types of groups: religious, community service, hobby-oriented, and many others.

Organizations and clubs often have a set of rules, usually unspoken, about how things function, so that people can get somewhat close but not too close. Thus, a MEM can practice defining and maintaining boundaries. MEM generally find this kind of structure helpful. It is important for a MEM to be careful about his impulse to want to make relationships more meaningful than they are, to get overinvolved too quickly, or to avoid connections for fear of being abused and exploited.

_∞_

Having reasonable boundaries and being clear about them is the key to turning unhealthy connections into better connections with Mom, Dad, sister, brother, and everybody else. This is easy to say and difficult for a MEM to do. This chapter has outlined some specific ways to help make it happen. In the next chapter, we consider another challenge for MEM: dating and marriage.

12 DIVORCE MOM AND DON'T MARRY SOMEONE LIKE HER
Guidelines for MEM on Dating and Marriage

A MEM seeking a satisfying committed relationship must face a necessary divorce from his mother. This divorce happens mainly by setting boundaries, as described in the previous chapter. However, it also involves examining his idealized image of his mother to discover how he holds her in his unconscious. A MEM needs to understand what sorts of expectations he may carry into his relationships. As noted in previous discussions, "the past is projected onto the present."

He also must be his "own man" while he considers commitment. He needs to become clear on his minimum requirements for a current or future relationship. He needs to write this down in a "Relationship Plan."

The Relationship Plan
A Relationship Plan provides a clear description of what kind of woman he wants in his life and what kind of relationship he would like to have with her. "I just want to be connected to somebody" isn't good enough. A MEM's Relationship Plan should especially include what he "must have." If his current

relationship is lacking in these bottom-line items, then he should focus on them as a priority in his discussions with her, in his individual therapy, and in couples counseling. If the MEM is still "just dating," he can use the Relationship Plan (and his left brain) to help him maintain awareness as he dates.

A Relationship Plan is a guide to what you are seeking. It is customized to you. By being explicit, you engage your left brain and don't leave yourself to the sometimes compulsive choices of your unconscious templates. Your plan should include an overall description of the relationship you envision. This description might begin with a "vision statement," a brief summary of your life situation and what you want; for example, "I am a single father with responsibility for my four-year-old daughter. I am looking for a life partner who will love me and my child." Then you might give more details under sections with titles such as: "What kind of relationship?" and "What kind of woman?"

After the description, there should be a reminder of the "red flags" that you need to look out for. These are shortcomings in a partner that you are particularly concerned about. It also makes sense to put down a few thoughts around compatibility that clarify the kind of commitment you want and the kind of life you want to lead. You should include your bottom line for the relationship, as described in Chapter 11. You might end your Relationship Plan with some final thoughts, perhaps under a heading like "Important to Keep in Mind," in the spirit of new healthy beliefs. See the box titled "New Beliefs for MEM" in Chapter 11. The basic principle in writing a Relationship Plan is to be clear about what is most important to you. The next box provides a summary.

I'm not focusing here on advice for casual dating. I'm think-

TEMPLATE FOR A RELATIONSHIP PLAN

1.   *Description*
  a.   What is your overall vision for your relationship? For example, "I'm looking for a life partner who will love me and my daughter."
  b.   What kind of relationship do you want? For example, "marriage and children." This can be as detailed as you want.
  c.   What kind of woman do you want? Whatever seems important.

2.   *Red flags.* Danger signals in the sense of shortcomings. For example, drinks too much, acts out sexually, mean-spirited, or any of the qualities of an unsafe person listed in the "Safe People—Unsafe People" box on page 207.

3.   *Compatibility.* How do her expectations for commitment match with yours? Does this woman want the same things in the relationship that you do? Are her plans for her life compatible with yours?

4.   *Bottom line.* Described in Chapter 11.

5.   *Important to keep in mind.* A few healthy beliefs. For example, "I am not being disloyal to my mother when I have a satisfying relationship with a woman."

ing more that you are seeking a serious relationship or that you are already in a serious relationship. The Relationship Plan becomes your resource for left-brain clarity: Is this relationship what you want? How does it need to improve? My MEM clients often have special trouble with bottom lines for their established relationships. If a man has been married for five years, he may be terrified of challenging his partner, and he may have no idea how to be decent, loving, and firm at the same time. Maybe an example will be helpful:

A MEM typically is going to need a partner who is willing to work with him and be patient as he makes progress in therapy. But if he is in a long-term relationship with a woman who is chronically dismissive, angry, dissatisfied, blaming, and narcissistic—perhaps someone like his mother—his emotional survival will require some changes. The bottom line is a way to clarify what's at stake.

He might present it to her something like this: "Our marriage [or relationship] is very important to me. I love you. However, I am being hurt by your never-ending criticism and dissatisfaction. I'm not going to be able to live with it much longer. In the spirit of giving us a chance, I want you to do some specific therapy work to see if this is a problem you can work on. If you can't make progress on this over the next three months, I'll have to leave you, even though that would be difficult.

"I'd like you to keep me abreast of what you're doing in the next few months. If you don't tell me that anything is going on, I'll assume nothing is happening, and I'll be making my decision to move in a different direction."

And then he prepares to go. He doesn't wait three months to begin making plans to leave. He needs to show her and himself that his bottom line is real.

How to Navigate a Relationship

A MEM has a tendency to let his unconscious templates control his relationships. His Disloyalty Bind leads him to choose women he can't commit to. This is one way he can stay loyal to Mom. Or he may have affairs and betray a woman who is good for him. In this way, he is also staying loyal to Mom. When an unconscious MEM does marry, he may continue to honor his Disloyalty Bind by marrying a surrogate for his mother—for instance, a critical, dependent, needy woman.

It is common for a MEM to be in a relationship but not be committed to the relationship. In this case, he should not remain with one foot in and one foot out. Here is the way I advise such MEM to give their current relationships a fair try without being "stuck" in them:

1. Can you get yourself to commit for a period of time to see if it works? Being even "temporarily" committed is different from just hanging out together. Let go of other women including "rainchecks," which cause you not to be fully present. See the next section.

2. Watch your own tendencies to project feelings. Are you projecting feelings about your mother onto her? Go to couples counseling to make sure you're communicating.

3. Engage your left brain in your decision-making process. Does she match your Relationship Plan? If so, stay put and work through your discomfort and fears of enmeshment. If not, let go of the impulse to be loyal and committed, even when it is not good for you.

4. Be ready to surrender perfection. Expecting to find a perfect partner is just another way to avoid commitment.

5. If a conscious and conscientious effort at commitment doesn't work, then make a definite decision to let go and move on. Turn from your failed relationship to a redoubled commitment *to yourself.* Follow the Relationship Plan I've already described and try again. Be aware of the five healthy courting stages discussed in Chapter 7 and make an effort to follow them.

The False Promise of the Affair

Committed relationships evoke the unconscious. For a MEM, an affair is a way to find relief from his struggle with commitment caused by his (unconscious) Disloyalty Bind. An affair falsely promises a MEM the possibility of burden-free intimacy. In an affair, he can simulate being open and intimate, because his enmeshment issues are not engaged. Therefore, the MEM can relax and have a good time. This "freedom," however, is just a temporary side effect of getting around the Disloyalty Bind. If the affair becomes a committed relationship, the Disloyalty Bind will reemerge.

Consider the way my client Robert fooled himself with an affair: At the beginning of his affair, Robert told himself, "Martha is the answer. I'm feeling things with her that I don't feel with my wife. I've never been so free. This is my true love."

But feelings can often be poor indicators of reality. Robert was feeling exhilarated because of his temporary escape from the burdens of his enmeshment. But his enmeshment issues were deep in his unconscious. They weren't going away just because he'd found a new woman. When he divorced his wife and became more committed to Martha, these issues reemerged. He projected his enmeshment feelings onto Martha. He lost his sense of freedom. Then *she* was the one he was in conflict with.

Robert had not gained anything by leaving his wife for Martha. In fact, he had suffered significant losses. He betrayed a wife and destroyed a family. His children suffered from his betrayal as well. His history of harming people was extended, including his long history of doing harm to himself. And he had the same problems with his new woman that he had had with the previous one: He felt engulfed and he wanted freedom.

Robert was not a cynical sexual hedonist or a compulsive womanizer. Rather, his problem lay in his willingness to believe his illusions of freedom and his fantasies of being saved by "the one" woman who was meant for him. It was a mutual illusion, since Martha was sharing it. The false promise of the affair is grounded in the false idea that our problems are outside of us, and, if we find the right person, we can be saved from the challenges of looking inward and making changes.

MEM in Love

There are two distinct personality types for MEM: placating MEM ("placators") and controlling MEM ("controllers"). This is a chapter of advice, and sometimes the correct advice for these two types of MEM needs to emphasize different things. Of the people we've met in Part One, Freddy is a placator, Doug is a controller, and Sonny falls somewhere between the two types. The personalities of many MEM are a blend of the extremes. For simplicity and clarity, however, discussing the extremes will be helpful.

A placator tends become enmeshed with his partner and lose his own identity. He appears conciliatory and passive, shy and vague, not fully "there." He is overly accommodating and neglects his own needs. After some time, he typically will find that being so accommodating burns him out and also brings up old resentments.

Controlling MEM are arrogant, authoritarian, rigid, demanding, and self-centered. They are terrified of losing themselves. They fear that they will once again be trapped: "I can't give in. Once I give in on something, I will have to give in on everything." These MEM cannot bear the give-and-take of healthy relationships.

A controlling MEM often uses affairs to help him keep his emotional distance. He obtains two additional "benefits" in having affairs: He is taking out on other women the anger he feels at his mother, and he is acting out the betrayal of his trust by his mother. We see the psychological power of having affairs: keeping emotional distance, expressing pent-up rage, and the compulsive repetition of damaged trust buried in the unconscious.

Note that some MEM avoid relationships entirely. Rather than being placating or controlling, they don't connect for friendship or romance. These socially isolated MEM never worked out a way to be disloyal to Mom and become their own independent men.

The Placating MEM

Placators tend to be compulsive and impetuous in romantic or sexual situations. They leave out the early to intermediate stages of courting (Chapter 7). They go from interest and attraction to sex or (fantasizing about) marriage too quickly. They neglect to consider whether they like the person they're dating.

The placator is quick to pick up on the problems and concerns of his partner and consider them his problems and concerns. If she says, "I've got to do . . . ," he will instinctively say, "Here, let me do that for you." I counsel my placator clients to refrain from doing that. This helping impulse feels familiar and normal to a placator. When I ask these MEM to spend some time instead pursuing their own interests, they often don't know what their own interests are.

Here is a story from one of my placator clients, which I taped and reproduce here with his permission:

I was probably twenty or twenty-one. I met a very attractive woman at a dance at the University of Michigan. She wasn't typical of the women I was drawn to. She was less needy. We went on a picnic. She was a mother, and she talked about her child. She was just making conversation, but I began to offer advice. It was automatic: Here was a woman; therefore, I was supposed to solve her problems. She said to me, "I don't need you to help me with this," or something like that. My shame came up big time. I ended the date as quickly as I could, and I never called her again. She may have wanted me to call her, but I couldn't because I was so ashamed. I thought I was supposed to take care of her problems, but she wanted nothing to do with it. She wanted to go out with me. She probably wanted to have sex, have fun, to date. I guess she was one of my many lost opportunities.

Placators continue to be placating after marriage, and the enmeshment of a placator with his wife tends to diminish their intimacy. If they have any sensitivity, both partners are likely to be dissatisfied. A husband needs to develop a healthy balance between devoting himself to the needs of his family and reserving some time and resources for himself. Placators find this balance difficult. They tend to hold nothing back for themselves. When they are close to a woman, they are trying to manage the feelings of being engulfed and overwhelmed by keeping her satisfied. Recall that people-pleasing and self-neglect are basic symptoms of MEM.

A placator can avoid these extremes by having boundaries and structure to "force" him to make some guilt-free time for himself. Something like "Tonight you and I will go out together.

Tomorrow's my night. The night after is yours." Such definition and structure will help him maintain a healthy balance in his relationship.

Here are my guidelines for placators who are dating. Consider writing down the answers to the questions to engage your conscious left-brain awareness. In dating, you should go slow and not commit too quickly: Keep space between dates, date others while you get to know someone, and postpone being sexual.

1. Track your natural reactions. Don't overly focus on taking care of her. Try to get in touch with how *you* feel.
   - Do you like this person?
   - Are you feeling emotionally safe, or do you feel the need to be on guard?
   - Are you feeling respected and validated?
2. Consider this woman's ability to work with you.
   - How does she respond when you state your preferences, your needs, and your desires? Is she willing to consider what you want?
   - Does she show an ability to listen to you and hear your concerns or complaints? Can she take them in and consider a possible need for her to change?
   - Does she have a process to accomplish changing herself, if need be? For example, would she consider individual therapy or marriage counseling?

The Controlling MEM
I usually encounter controllers after they are married and unhappy. They come to me criticizing their wives, having affairs, and wanting a divorce. They wonder why they are so lonely.

Let's consider a controller, William, with whom I am currently working. In his own words, he requires his wife to be "submissive" to him. He's dominant, and he wanted it that way. Except that now he wants to leave. He's had a number of affairs, and he thinks the affairs reflect some kind of reality. Of course they don't. This is the false promise of the affair, already discussed.

His wife has discovered his affairs, and this has precipitated his crisis. That's why he's come to therapy. He had never before considered what kind of person he wanted to be married to, even though he has been married to Connie for twenty years and they have two children.

In therapy, he asks, "What do I want? I've got a relationship I don't like, because she's dependent on me, and I've made her that way. And how do I change that? Do I have to divorce her to change it?"

I've advised him to stop playing the role of "daddy" and to begin to see his wife as more of an equal. That's a struggle for him. He feels comfortable with her submissive role, because it reverses the role he had with his mother. It helps him not to feel so helpless with a woman, which is what he is defending against.

A controller is frightened by women. He needs to be in control, because he doesn't want ever again to feel the engulfment, the fear, the panic, and the rage that he once felt as a boy being forced to be submissive to his mother. He's likely to choose someone who is dependent on him, not just financially but emotionally.

Both the placator and the controller exhibit strong caretaking qualities. However, the controller caretakes his wife by taking charge, while the placator tries to be perfectly responsive to accomplish the same goal. Both want to keep the peace and maybe get a little love.

Both types of MEM eventually gain some sense that they've never been authentic. Often they feel they've created marriages they never really wanted. These MEM married out of their unconscious templates, which were developed to defend against the enmeshment with their mothers. While they were dating, they didn't stop to ask themselves "Do I like her? Do I respect her?" They focused instead on "Can I keep her placated or under control?"

William is having a true personal crisis. He doesn't want to continue the affairs. He cares enough about his wife that he doesn't want to hurt her. He's not so narcissistic that I can't guide him to take a look at himself.

I encourage him to talk about how he truly feels and to give up the sort of con he uses with his wife. He thinks he wants to leave the marriage, but when he goes to marriage counseling, he pretends he's trying to work it out. He tells Connie what he thinks she wants to hear, both because he doesn't want to hurt her and because he doesn't want to have to deal with her anger and disappointment. In this, his behavior is indistinguishable from that of a placator.

I usually evaluate the partner as part of my process of individual treatment. I want to get the woman's point of view, particularly if the man is narcissistic or sexually addicted. In either case, he's not going to tell me the whole story. From William's description, I was expecting Connie to be a snarling monster. Instead, she was beautiful, attentive, sensitive, and concerned. William reports that she has been mean and retaliatory. So she clearly has some problems, but she isn't his implacable foe. That way of looking at her is his projection of his inner representation of his mother.

I've let William know I have some concerns and doubts

about his plan to leave Connie. "Why are you leaving?" I've asked him. "Write down the reasons you want to leave, and write down the losses that you expect to experience." I had him visualize the year after the divorce, sitting in his apartment alone. "How does it feel? Is this what you want? Go there. Imagine it." He started crying. He's facing some significant losses. He would certainly miss his children.

The main guidelines I try to teach controllers like William are:

1. Know yourself.
   - Learn to be authentic. Get in touch with how you really feel and what you really believe.
   - Work on your anger and fear in a therapeutic setting.
2. Be honest.
   - Share the important and relevant parts of who you are. Don't try to manipulate her or manage her feelings.
   - Give up your affairs. Don't leave for another woman, either in reality or in fantasy.
   - Confront your self-centeredness and narcissism. Learn to give rather than to take.

Inappropriate Loyalty and Unsafe People

The enmeshment experience lays a foundation in MEM for inappropriate loyalty. We saw this in Chapter 8 around Arthur's work dilemma. When a work or social or marriage situation is bad, MEM tend to become more loyal and won't consider leaving, even after reasonable steps have not produced improvements. This tendency is why it is so important for MEM to make a point of developing and honoring bottom lines for each of their relationships.

The enmeshment experience also desensitizes MEM to people who are selfish and exploitative. Therefore, MEM often miss the cues that someone could potentially harm or exploit them. They learn not to consider their own feelings or reactions to people. They have trouble knowing that they are with a safe person, and they can be remarkably unaware of signals of danger. See the next box for some guidelines.

How to Have a Conscious Relationship

A man with a family will certainly organize his life around the needs of his wife and children, but a typical placator will have trouble holding back anything for himself. The controller goes to the opposite extreme by separating himself from his sense of

SAFE PEOPLE	UNSAFE PEOPLE
1. Tend to express their feelings in moderate and reasonable ways.	1. Tend not to reveal their feelings, or, if they do, it's in extreme ways. They either threaten, so that you will feel intimidated, or they become martyrs to make you feel guilty.
2. Tend to be compassionate, understanding, and empathic when you share your feelings.	2. Don't show much empathy. They have difficulty being sensitive to how it feels to be in another person's shoes.
3. Show interest in you, what you are doing, and how you're feeling.	3. Are self-focused and self-interested. They make most topics of conversation about themselves.

SAFE PEOPLE	UNSAFE PEOPLE
4. Are willing to negotiate the relationship. They let you know if they feel there is a problem between the two of you. They are interested in knowing how you feel about their behavior, if there seems to be a problem.	4. Don't negotiate in relationships. They do not have good relationship histories. They have only a few friends or only subservient or dominant friends.
5. Are clear about who they are, what they believe, and their intentions.	5. Are vague about their motives, intentions, and commitments. They blame others when they are misunderstood.
6. Feel good to be around. You know where you stand with them.	6. Don't "feel right" to you. For example, narcissists will tend to make you feel inadequate and unsure of yourself, in response to their need to dominate and their inability to recognize you as a separate person.

responsibility and becoming detached. Both of these patterns—not holding back and becoming detached—are destructive to relationships and families. Placators and controllers should make their particular patterns the central focus of their therapy.

Both types of MEM should go slow in dating and make a special effort to decide if they like a woman before committing to her. They should be explicit about what they want by writing a Relationship Plan. They should become aware of their patterns of behavior through therapy and, if they are already in a committed relationship, through couples counseling.

A MEM wanting a satisfying relationship with a woman must accomplish three tasks:

1. The MEM needs to free himself from the control of his enmeshment experiences. A MEM is so accustomed to taking care of the woman's needs, or taking charge, that he hasn't developed a sense that there is somebody there for him. He needs to believe that a safe loving connection is possible and that he doesn't need to protect himself by placating or controlling. He needs to stop escaping through fantasies or a new woman.

2. The MEM and his partner must address his tendency to project his feelings from the past into the relationship. The MEM intuitively will feel the need to pull away from, or keep his distance from, his partner, when in fact it's often his mother that he wants to escape.

3. The following question must be resolved: Are the MEM's enmeshment issues getting in the way of a potentially great relationship, or should the relationship end, because this man and this woman are fundamentally not good for each other?

✑

This chapter and the previous one have focused on the needs of the MEM: how he can have better relationships with parents, siblings, partners, and others. The next chapter directly addresses the needs of partners of MEM. It includes the answers to questions I am frequently asked about relationship issues and therapy.

13 SHOULD I STAY OR SHOULD I GO?

And Other Questions Asked by Women Involved with MEM

Partners of MEM ask me many questions: Should I stay or should I go? What should I do and avoid doing to make the relationship better? How do I get him into therapy, and what do I do when he is in therapy? What if I'm involved with a married MEM who wants to leave his wife and marry me? And so on. I answer all these questions and others in this chapter.

But first, are you really involved with a MEM? The previous questionnaires were from the point of view of the MEM. This one considers how things look to the partner. Answer each question yes or no. The more questions with a yes answer, the more likely it is that you are involved with a MEM.

Are You Involved with a MEM?

1. Does he let his mother interfere in your relationship?
2. Does he do what his mother tells him to do, even when he should have consulted with you first?
3. After a visit or phone call with his mother, is he irritable, critical, or distant with you?

4. Does he seem to go out of his way to keep you and his mother apart?

5. Is his mother critical of you when speaking to him or even directly to you?

6. Does he have difficulty making simple commitments, like going to a movie or dinner?

7. Does he seem touchy about not wanting to be "controlled"?

8. Does he often say things like "don't pressure me" when you attempt to bring up the future of your relationship?

9. Has his level of interest and attention for you steadily decreased for no apparent reason?

10. Do you often feel unsure about your importance to him, and are you rebuffed when you attempt to discuss it with him?

Should You Stay or Should You Go?

To make a good decision on whether to stay or go, the partner of a MEM must be realistic and courageous. Being realistic means knowing things won't "just change." Empty promises and wishful thinking won't do the job. Being courageous means being able to risk ending the relationship. Your core fear may be that your MEM doesn't love you enough to change. However, being clear about what must happen for you to stay and what will cause you to go can strengthen or save your relationship.

Creating this clarity is what the bottom line is about. The bottom line for the partner of a MEM is basically the same as described in Chapter 11. However, the concern for the partner of a MEM is most often around the issue of having a definite commitment. When the man is just not willing to change and be available for commitment, in spite of all your best efforts to be patient, you may need your bottom line to clarify for him and you what your boundaries are. Your bottom line should not be used to control or coerce a commitment from him but rather used as a limit for yourself as well as for him. It is a respectful reminder of your needs, not a threat.

You might say "I've really enjoyed our relationship. I like you. However, I've found it difficult that you put your mother before me on a regular basis, letting her interrupt our special time and canceling dates with me when she's asked for last-minute help. I can't live with that. I think we can still make things better. I'd like to ask you to do some therapy around your relationship with your mother. If you can't make progress on this over the next month, I can't stay with you. I don't want to nag you, so I'm not going to be reminding you about this. I need you to show me you're taking this problem seriously." He is now responsible. He knows what to do to keep you in his life. In that month's time, you're preparing your exit. You'll be doing things like finding another place to live, getting friends to be supportive, and arranging to be financially independent. You're not waiting to see how it comes out. You're preparing to back up your statement with practical action.

I also recommend that partners of MEM develop their own version of a Relationship Plan (see Chapter 12), whether they are merely hoping for a serious relationship or have been married for years.

You could consider including in your bottom line and Relationship Plan versions of the traits given in the next box. These qualities are basic to a MEM's ability to have a relationship at all, much less have a good relationship with you. You can also consider what type of MEM you are connected to: placating or controlling (see Chapter 12). If you try to get your placator into therapy before he burns himself out, he will most likely comply, if only to please you. After that, success will depend on his ability to emerge from denial. A controller can be charming and exciting, but when he begins to feel dissatisfied, his first thought is to find a new woman. With either type of MEM, you are looking for evidence that he is willing to become conscious of the problems associated with his mother. Thus, a history of personal reflection is a good sign.

QUALITIES TO LOOK FOR IN YOUR MEM

1. He is reliable and does what he says he is going to do.

2. He is not too charming and solicitous too soon.

3. He is willing to negotiate with you. He isn't always focused on himself. He is considerate if you feel slighted.

4. He isn't always placating and conciliatory to you. He shows preferences and has boundaries.

5. He is clear about what he believes, what he wants, and where he is going (family, career, etc.) without being rigid about it. This clarity allows you to make informed decisions about how, and if, you want to work something out with him.

6. He is mature and responsible. Play is important to him, but it is not his primary focus.

7. He shows commitment in significant areas of his life.

8. He has a quality of humility, and he can be vulnerable with you. He seems willing to seek outside help in personal matters, if needed.

A MEM's capacity for clarity and connection will depend on his degree of separation from his mother. The more separate he is (or is willing to become), the more capacity to commit he will have. If your MEM doesn't make progress on his enmeshment issues, there are basically only two choices for you: accept it or break up. How can you tell if he is making progress? He should, over the time period of (say) a year, make his mother less primary and you more primary, so that you don't continue to doubt your place in his life. He should begin to stand up to his mother if she criticizes you or directly interferes in the relationship. He should look at his own behavior in a therapeutic setting, end his affairs, and work to stop his addictions.

Of course, your own willingness and ability to stay with him over his long period of recovery is a factor in how you set your bottom line. Also, if you find yourself ignoring reality and not taking care of yourself, perhaps focusing on his needs only, you need to seek professional help for yourself. Your first concern should be: Is the relationship working for you?

Questions I'm Frequently Asked by Women Involved with MEM

Partners of MEM often come to see me seeking basic information. Here are the questions I'm most commonly asked, along with my answers.

Isn't it a good sign for a man to be close to his mother? Yes. Normally, it is a good sign. When a man is close to his mother, this often suggests that he will be able to have a good connection with a romantic partner. But a MEM is different. The place where a romantic partner should go in a MEM's heart is blocked by his mother. It isn't accessible to you.

Is the reason he's backing off because I'm pressuring him? No. It's because of a MEM's commitment phobia and his unconscious confusion of you with his mother. However, if you have become angry and demanding in your attempts to get him to commit, then you may be helping to provoke his withdrawal. It would probably be useful for you to work on another strategy to express your wishes for commitment. For example, you could calmly and lovingly clarify your bottom line with him.

How can I get him to be more committed to me? You can't. His ambivalence isn't about you, and you can't fix it directly. However, extending some understanding and patience (providing he is working on his MEM issues) will help him see you in a positive and safe light rather than as an object of his projected feelings.

Should I pressure him to face his MEM issues? No, you shouldn't. The more you pressure him and confront him, the more you will cause him to feel that you are his mother, smothering him and limiting his autonomy. However, you may need to establish (or reestablish) your bottom line with him, so that both he and you understand that, if he cannot change, you cannot stay. Be honest and loving, but don't pressure him endlessly. Your bottom line relieves you of the need to constantly remind him.

Should I try to be understanding and helpful? If you are in a negotiated relationship in which you are working on his MEM issues together, extending him some gentleness and understanding could be very useful for both of you. However, be careful not to turn helpfulness and understanding into a form of denial, to avoid the conflict of letting him know how you feel.

What should I do when he lets his mother interfere with us? Don't take a direct confrontational approach. You need to address the problem calmly. Let him know what your boundaries are. Explain but don't explode. When the boundary is violated, be clear about what has happened. For example, say to him: "I'm uncomfortable that once again you've let your mother interrupt us. I've asked you not to take calls when we're on a date. I think I'm going to have to ask you to take me home." You could also choose not to make an issue of it at the time but bring it up later, for example, in a joint therapy session.

How do I have a relationship with my MEM's mother? You have to keep in mind that she's going to see you as competition and someone who is trying to "steal" her son. You are a threat. Therefore, you can't have a normal relationship with her, whether she is your mother-in-law or just your boyfriend's mother. You'll have to keep a respectful distance. In fact, she may be overtly or covertly antagonistic toward you and be working to undermine your relationship with her son. You and your MEM should explicitly discuss together how you are going to handle this. It's okay to ask him to tell his mother that he isn't going to welcome negative comments about you. If he is unwilling to do this, then his loyalty remains with her and not you. This is not a good sign for your relationship.

Sometimes, after you have established a long-term commit-ted relationship with her son, say a marriage, the mother will relent, give in to reality, and decide to try to make a positive connection with you. You could remain open to this opportu-nity but keep some respectful distance. Don't attempt to be overly close to counter your fear that she will reject you or that you won't appear to be "nice." An enmeshing mother will have an impulse to be meddling, if you allow her to get too close.

What if he's involved with other women? It isn't uncommon for a MEM to "keep in touch" with other women, as part of his pat-tern of avoiding full commitment. If you suspect he's involved with another woman, you need to ask him about it. Some con-trollers have a life pattern of lying and womanizing. If you have a clear sense that he's seeing someone, but he's not confirming it, then you may need to trust your intuition. Establish a clear bot-tom line, and, if things don't get better, end the relationship.

If you suspect he's involved with other women but you are unwilling to bring it up with him, then you should go to therapy to discover what is preventing you from taking care of yourself. You most likely have some issue that prevents you from dealing with betrayals of your trust. See the discussion in Chapter 8 on "betrayal bonds."

When should I decide to end the relationship? Three situations should cause you to end a relationship with a MEM:

1. Your MEM refuses to acknowledge or do anything about his relationship to his mother.
2. He is involved with other women and refuses to give them up and seek help.
3. Your own personal history or inner resources won't allow you to tolerate the long journey of healing with him.

Questions About Therapy

Here are the most common questions I get asked by the partners of MEM about therapy, along with the suggestions I usually give.

How do I get my MEM into therapy? First, acknowledge your differences. Say to him "You and I have some differences of opinion about your relationship with your mother and how it affects our relationship. I love you, and I'd like our relationship to continue. What if we go to see somebody who can help us sort this out? We can get an unbiased third-party opinion." This way you're not saying you think he's pathological. You're not confronting him about his behavior with his mother, other than to say that there's a difference of opinion. You're not making him admit that he's "wrong." Here you will be most likely taking a more neutral position with him than you feel. You might ask him if he would agree to six sessions with the therapist, just to see if it would help the two of you to talk. This way you're using the neutral language to "talk about" it rather than to "change" it.

Second, you should find a couples therapist and make the call to set up the appointment at a mutually convenient time, so he doesn't have an excuse not to go. If he doesn't want to go with you at any time, then go by yourself to discuss the situation. He may join you at a later session.

Finally, it will probably make sense for him to go to individual therapy. The story of Sonny and Anne in Chapter 1 illustrates this process.

If he acknowledges the problem from the start, then having him go for individual therapy right away would be appropriate, with the option of joint therapy after he gets clearer about what he's dealing with. More typically, he's not admitting he has a problem, and you're coaxing him to come in with you to talk about the "difference of opinion."

How do I prepare for our first joint session? You will naturally be concerned about going into your first joint session. If you're starting out in individual therapy and then going on to joint therapy, your therapist should help you understand what should happen that will be good for you, your partner, and the relationship. Explore with your therapist the possibilities for that first session. The next questions and responses will also give you a sense of what to expect.

What will happen in joint therapy? The therapist will most likely start out the first session by asking both of you to express your differences as statements about what you feel or observe. The well-worn formulas are: "When you do *that,* I feel *this.* When I bring *that* up, *this* happens." A good couples therapist will teach you this way of presenting your issues right at the start. Your feelings about your relationship can be brought up, but the self-owning style doesn't fuel his defenses.

Harville Hendrix describes this approach in his book *Getting the Love You Want: A Guide for Couples.* You don't say, "He's too close to his mother. He's a mama's boy. He's a baby." Instead, you say, "I'm concerned that the relationship my husband has with his mother interferes with our marriage. We have a difference of opinion about that. I'd like to share what it feels like and looks like from my perspective."

In spite of preparation, sometimes a couple will just disgorge complaints in the session. To some degree, this is good. But a storm of ten years' worth of complaints is overwhelming. Also, it likely will contain issues from your past that you are unfairly projecting onto your partner. Your grievances should be sorted, not just dumped, when you do a couples dialogue.

What should I do with my justified anger? I know this is tough, but you must learn to use your anger constructively. If you express your disappointment by blaming, he's just going to go into his shell and not come out. Try to take a step back and see it from his point of view: He's in a bind. He's not the man who "won't see it" but the man who "can't see it." This was the case for Sonny in Chapter 1. If you make a big point of the fact that he's got a problem, then you will win the battle of expressing your feelings but lose the war of making your relationship better.

The therapist should not allow either of you to attack, criticize, or indulge in putdowns. We have good evidence that successful relationships are characterized by high levels of positive exchange, even in disagreements, as described in *The Seven*

Principles for Making Marriage Work by John Gottman and Nan Silver.

An attacked person becomes defensive and isn't available for compromise or change. On the other hand, if the therapist invalidates your concerns, that's not helpful either. You should be able to express all your concerns and feelings. The therapist should encourage you to do this while discouraging attacking and raging. Otherwise, find another therapist.

However, your anger is important. You can take advantage of its energy. Use it to set boundaries. Use it to get clarity. Use it to motivate yourself to write your Relationship Plan.

What if I just can't do it? I try to stop it, but the flow of my past complaints just keeps coming. What then? If you're unable to get past the intensity of your resentment and anger and be constructive with it, it's time for you to go into individual therapy. Work specifically on presenting your grief and anger in a responsible and constructive way. Perhaps your relationship has provoked feelings from the past that are getting projected onto the present. The more intense and repetitive the reaction is, the more likely something is being triggered in the right brain, expressing old pent-up feelings. These intense and repetitive reactions are diagnostic indicators (red flags) to therapists that the response is coming from the past.

You're probably tapping into something from your childhood where someone has hurt or betrayed you. Since the current energy is directed at your MEM partner, the past energy may be about your father. But it could also be a displacement from an enmeshed relationship with your own mother. You tell your partner, then you have to tell him again, and again, and again. The reason you can't let it go in the present is because the person you need to hear it isn't there. When you feel like whatever your partner does isn't good enough—even though he shows evidence of changing—you may be projecting from the past.

To help establish a point of view that includes the past when I am counseling couples about this, I might say: "It sounds like you're really angry and can't let this go, and you're locked into something. What is it you think you're locked into? Are you frightened he's never going to deal with this?" Then I might turn to the MEM: "Can you see how much she cares about your relationship? Can you offer her any comfort that you're ready to look at this?"

If he is ready to look at himself and work on his MEM issues, but you still can't accept his attempt at face value, I might ask you to consider what makes it difficult for you. I would ask you if you could convert your *complaints* into *concerns* by saying to your MEM: "I'm concerned that your relationship with your mother is going to get in the way," and "I notice when *that* happens, *this* is how you treat me." This change in point of view is different from angry, critical reactions.

I understand that I'm asking a lot from you. You may have had years of dealing with the MEM's frustrating and infuriating behaviors. It isn't unreasonable that you would become enraged and despondent. You may feel it is ten years too late, and you are so resentful that you can't shake it off. This is a key decision point for you. If you can't try to let go of your position of perpetual resentment, then you might find it difficult to grow with the positive changes that are happening. You may need to leave in order to avoid a chronically distant, antagonistic, or contemptuous relationship and to give yourself a chance to grieve and start over.

When He Gets You and His Mother Mixed Up

When he responds to you with the anger, withdrawal, and ambivalence that he once felt as a boy—or more likely that he couldn't allow himself to feel as a boy—he is getting you and his mother mixed up. Sonny from Chapter 1 was doing this to Anne. How could this happen? Let my client Mike tell you what the experience feels like in his own words.

> *I was dating Alice. We had our difficulties, but things were going pretty well. We would get together two or three times a week. We would hold hands and make love and go to dinner and have fun and go to a movie. So I remember very distinctly one day. We made love the day before. We held hands. We had done whatever we usually did. And in between that date and the next time I saw her, which was only a couple of days, my mother called me. It was one of those guilt-filled, what-did-I-do-to-deserve-this lectures. I was used to them, and I didn't think it affected me very much. But then Alice went to hold my hand as we were walking down the street, and I no more wanted to hold her hand than I wanted to jump off a cliff. I literally could not do it. I found it completely disgusting. I felt angry at her, and I didn't know why. All of a sudden everything had shifted, and I couldn't help it. We broke up soon after that.*

Mike's story is a clear description of the way an encounter with Mother can affect a MEM's feelings for his girlfriend or wife. But he might be "triggered" like this even if he doesn't get a phone call from Mom. The encounter might be in his head.

How do you know whether he's had this kind of mental visit from Mom? The best signal is in a sudden change in his feelings, an "unmotivated" rapid withdrawal or outburst.

Your main defense against your MEM's projecting his feelings is *awareness that he is unleashing on you feelings he has for his mother.* Your awareness can help, so that you don't absorb the full force of his projecting. Instead, both you and he can learn to put it in its proper perspective. When he is projecting, you might tell him: "I feel hurt when you say that. I have done nothing to provoke it. If you'd like to discuss it at another time, let me know." I sometimes suggest to clients that they imagine holding up one of those Plexiglas police shields to fend off the projecting.

Awareness also lets you show him some sensitivity and gentleness while he regains himself after his encounter with his mother. The benefit of gentleness, as opposed to pressure or confrontation, is that it will help him differentiate you from his mother. Ideally, he will be aware of his tendency to project. Then both of you can be on the same side as he recovers.

Couples therapy is a good place to clear the air after an encounter where he has made you his mother. If he is unaware of what he's doing, he needs to become aware of it. Increased awareness is a powerful healing force.

If he doesn't seek help, there is little chance that your relationship is going to change for the better. The stories of Sonny and Anne (Chapter 1), Sam and Carol (Chapter 5), and Warren and Judy (Chapter 6) are all examples of how various couples successfully approached becoming more aware and thereby getting better. Tony and Elizabeth (Chapter 3) broke up because Tony couldn't deal with his issues and Elizabeth wasn't willing to live in a crippled relationship. Freddy (Chapter 7) came to clarity and decided he had to get a divorce when Angela wouldn't grow with him.

Your Own Part of the Difficulties

It isn't uncommon for the partner of a MEM to also have her own issues. I sometimes discover that the partner of a MEM was enmeshed herself, with her mother or father or both, and she may be avoiding the feelings of her enmeshment by projecting them onto her partner.

It is a cliché of relationship therapy that the individual issues of partners are "chosen" to create the greatest potential for conflict but also the greatest potential for healing. This seeming paradox is acknowledged by Harville Hendrix in his Imago approach to relationship therapy. For example, a woman could marry a man who has some of the negative characteristics of her father, after having sworn that she would never do that. In turn, the man has chosen a woman who has some of the worst characteristics of his mother. Being married to each other leads to conflicts, but these conflicts are messages from the past that clarify what damage in each partner needs healing. Imago therapy makes this meshing of issues between partners a cornerstone of the recovery process, as described in Hendrix's book *Getting the Love You Want*.

Integrity and pragmatism suggest that you consider your own contributions to the issues that are limiting your relationship. It is always a good idea to look into your own background—and your own relationship history—for contributing sources of difficulty. Rarely does the "blame" for relationship difficulties belong entirely to one of the partners, although it is common for the other partner to think so.

The False Promise of Being "The Other Woman"

Remember Martha from the previous chapter, Robert's "other woman"? She believed Robert would settle down with her because he was such a sweetie and he really loved her. This was illusion. Powerful unconscious forces were in action, and she could work no such magic change in her MEM.

She had gotten a false picture of his availability. He'd proclaimed the undying love for her that he couldn't have with his wife. What she didn't see was that she would become the woman he had to escape from after his divorce, when she began to want him to commit to her. The devoted, passionate lover was only the mask of Robert's False Self.

The consequences were bad for Martha in a number of ways. She helped to cause significant damage by hurting an innocent woman and her children. She didn't get what was promised her. Robert had told her she was "the one" woman for him, but he wasn't so sure when she became available. Their shared illusion of love and freedom collapsed under the uncompromising realities of the Disloyalty Bind.

Make It Better or Let It End

Don't wait passively hoping things will get better. Take action to move your relationship forward. Being proactive will lead you to the answer. Either your relationship will become more fulfilling, or you will understand that it needs to end. Coming to either conclusion will be better than being stuck and not knowing what you can do about it. All the stories in Chapters 1 to 7 describe how people confronted this stay-or-go decision.

Seek competent professional help. Your man's MEM issues are barriers to communication and action. You may find it impossible to get past them on your own.

Be excruciatingly explicit with him about what you want. Write it in your Relationship Plan and go over it with him. Compromise is okay as long as you are not betraying your core needs. Include time limits for progress. The fear that he doesn't love you enough to change should not be a barrier. Keeping a bad relationship is often worse than ending it.

Be active in pursuing your own personal growth. The key factor for creating a successful relationship is how willing and able you both are to work on your issues in a therapeutic framework.

⟡

Since so much of this book has been about the dysfunction of mothers and fathers, I feel it is important to address the topic of what good parenting looks like in the next chapter.

14 GUARDIAN ANGELS
Parenting Is a Spiritual Mission

...the highest safeguard for the physical, mental, and spiritual heath of the child is not primarily the attention paid to the child but the unrestricted love of the parents for each other.

—HENRI NOUWEN, *Intimacy*

Parents have a spiritual mandate to be guardian angels in the lives of their children. When parents lose sight of their spiritual mission and use their children selfishly, the children may develop emotional wounds that are significant and permanent. Parents must be willing to do whatever they need to do, including therapy, to rise to the occasion as if it were the most important task they have—which, of course, it is.

Mother-son enmeshment is an inversion of the purpose and significance of parenting. A lonely, angry, wounded mother feeds on her son's love to solve her emotional problems. She clings to this "solution," even as her child struggles to resist smothering. The enmeshing mother violates the essence of her spiritual mandate.

The father also has a sacred responsibility. He must not abandon his post. If he sees enmeshment developing, he must intervene. He must work with his wife to maintain the marital bond that protects their son. It is his part to say "Wait a minute. We have a responsibility here. We can't just do what we want."

Nothing in this chapter should be interpreted to mean that I don't think parents should parent. Children need guidance and limits. Parents as angels still set boundaries for the behavior of their children. They still say no when that's needed. Being "permissive" is not what I'm talking about here.

My point is spiritual: The *meaning* of parenting is angelic. Children are not "found treasure" provided for exploitation. Parents are trusted with the physical, emotional, and spiritual stewardship of their children.

In this chapter, we consider how a mother can avoid enmeshing her son. I give explicit advice for both the mother and the father. There are two basic guidelines for the mother: She should learn to be attuned to her son as a separate person from her, and she should take care of her own needs without using her son for emotional support. The father helps the mother be more aware if she is drifting into enmeshment without knowing it. He offers her emotional support. And, most important, he helps his son by remaining present for him.

The Enmeshing Mother and the Good-Enough Mother

The enmeshing mother—having been neglected, abused, or enmeshed herself—personalizes the reactions of her infant. She's reactive rather than attentive. She feels distress at meeting her infant's needs. She feels a distinct sense of limited resources. She says to her baby, "You're crying too much. I just fed you. I don't know what to do with you. What do you want now?" Even with a newborn she feels a kind of jealous competitiveness, as if the baby is taking something away from her. The enmeshing mother shows little tolerance for her infant's needs. In her frustration she feels, *I only have so much to give, and I just gave it to you.* It is "always about her" rather than about her child.

A number of authors use the phrase "good enough" to suggest that a mother, father, or family doesn't have to be "perfect" as long as the parenting is essentially healthy. Psychologists have many examples of destructive parenting in their case files. Good-enough families are not characterized by these destructive patterns and produce children who are not emotionally damaged. I will use the phrase from time to time in its popular sense, without attempting to give it a more clinical definition.

The good-enough mother can tolerate her infant's demands much longer than the enmeshing mother. The good-enough mother is more attuned and attentive to helping the infant regulate distress. For the good-enough mother, the infant's cries become a language she's trying to understand: "Are you hungry? Are you wet?" A good mother can be provoked; all parents become taxed at some point. But "I'm tired; I can't do this anymore" is different from "I just gave you something, and you want more! Stop bothering me." The enmeshing mother feels impatience with her infant's never-ending needs.

The enmeshing mother wants the child's attention, and she has a harsh, indignant reaction when the child doesn't give it to her. If the child is crying, the mother is distressed. Her reaction is "Don't you love Mommy?" When the child is cooing and attentive, the mother is using him to calm herself. Her sense of reassurance that she is okay is out of proportion to the mere fact of a contented baby.

To some degree, such a responsive mood is normal, natural, and healthy for a mother. It becomes pathological when the mother is expressing and demonstrating (1) chronic and repetitive impatience, along with a sense of limited emotional resources, and (2) a sense that she needs the child's adoration more than she's able to adore the child. She is distressed, even angry, when she perceives the child isn't giving it to her.

Later, when the toddler wants to explore, the enmeshing mother will be very distressed with him for that. She cannot let him wander away. She needs him close to her. She says things like: "Don't go too far. You're going to get hurt. Stay close to mommy." She says these things even though the toddler is in no danger. As we have already summarized in Chapter 8, he will feel guilt and shame as she insists that he attune to her needs. He learns to feel unsure of himself, when he wants to follow his natural impulse to be curious and to investigate away from mom. He becomes inhibited and timid. John Bowlby, a developmental psychiatrist, has done extensive research on mothers as a safe haven for an exploring child. He observes that, because an enmeshed boy is discouraged from exploring the world away from his mother, he ends up believing that he will never be able to make his way on his own (paraphrasing from *A Secure Base,* p. 150).

The guiding principle for taking care of a child is *being attuned*. The mother should attune to the child's needs rather than her own neediness.

What can a mother do to be more attuned to her baby? I often recommend parenting classes or books, so that the mother will have a clear sense of what the baby needs. However, if she is experiencing chronic feelings of grief, anger, or resentment that prevent her from responding to what she knows her baby needs, then I recommend therapy. It can also be helpful to seek support and mentoring from mothers who seem to find attunement natural and enjoyable.

When the child becomes a toddler, it is helpful to realize that all children go through a process of needing to come and go. They need to boldly leave their parents' security and then be able to return and regress. A mother should let her son have that regression without exploiting it for her own needs, and she should allow him to leave again later when he needs to. She may want to find support by talking with a friend or therapist about how her son's separation makes her feel. Even good-enough mothers will feel loss as their sons move away.

The good-enough mother is more tolerant of her child's exploring. She keeps a close eye on him without inhibiting his responses. She might say, "I really enjoyed how you learned to play with your friend." Or, "I liked the way you went off to look at the butterflies in the garden." She takes delight in his growing independence, and also she allows him to come back and seek comfort from her. She cuddles him when he feels needy or scared, and she opens her arms to let him go when he wants to go exploring again.

Some days your little boy will forget how to tie his shoes, and you should just take that in stride. Then, when he wants to go out conquering the world again, you are going to be reminded how soothing his regressive dependency felt to you. It will pull on your longing to use him to fill that empty part of you. You must resist it and go elsewhere to get your needs met. Remind yourself that the cost to your little boy is too great, and besides, it will never be enough to fill your emptiness. You have the right, the need, and the responsibility to heal yourself. And you can do this without exploiting your son's dependency.

How Can I Avoid Enmeshing My Son?

I was appearing on a local TV show to discuss mother-son en-meshment. The studio audience was small, so the TV people sent in some of the technical and administrative staff to fill it out. I finished my part and was leaving when Sally, who was one of the staff people, stopped me.

"Please," she said. "I need to talk with you."

There were tears in her eyes. We found a quiet place to sit.

"My husband was an alcoholic. He got in a fight at work, and they fired him. Then he sat around all day drinking beer and didn't get another job. So I threw him out."

I nodded.

"Charlie is so sweet. He's five. I always say he's my best friend. We do things together. He'll listen when I talk. He doesn't understand, but he listens. We go to McDonald's and then a movie. He doesn't mind if it's something I like."

"Charlie's your little boy?"

She nodded. "You said he's not supposed to be my best friend. That it would hurt him if he was. Will it really?"

"It's better for him if you're just his mother, not his friend. You have to take care of him and take care of yourself sepa-rately."

"How do I do that?"

∽

I'm asked Sally's question by mothers of boys of various ages, but especially young boys. I generally give some version of the following guidelines.

A little boy will naturally want to take care of his mother, especially if he sees she is unhappy and lonely and has no one else. He will want to do this, but if you depend on him for your emotional support, he may be harmed taking on a job he's not prepared for. If you sense this may be happening, you need to tell him explicitly, "It isn't your job to take care of me." You should repeat this whenever he tries to do it. Reassure him: "Mommy is okay. You don't have to take care of me." This will be difficult, because it is nice to have a little boy earnestly trying to be helpful. Saying it out loud reinforces the message for you and calms his concerns as well.

Despite my warnings in the previous paragraph, it is important that you keep a sense of perspective in responding to your son's concern for your welfare. If you feel secure that you're not depending on your son to fulfill your unmet emotional needs, his concern for you is healthy and does not need to be discouraged. It is his way of learning empathy. What you need to avoid is depending on him to keep you feeling emotionally okay.

A mother should make a point of being aware of what is going on with her son. Is he doing okay at school, socially and academically? Is he home alone often, or does he have things to do? Does he get "sick" a lot and want to stay home from school? Does he seem overly focused on you (his mother)? He probably won't say much about any of this, even if asked, although he should be asked about it anyway. The key for the mother is to be as aware as possible. One caution: Be aware of your son's verbal or nonverbal cues that your questions are starting to be intrusive. Be respectful of his right to privacy, both in the bathroom and in his head.

It is natural that a single mother will have to deal with loneliness. She should see this as a need for *adult* companionship, something to take care of with other adults. If there is no adult companionship available at home, she can look to find it at church, at clubs, at other activities adults socialize around, even at work. Friendly acquaintances can be a big help in lifting the weight of loneliness.

When a mother is spending time with her little boy, she should focus on his activities and his needs, whether it is homework or a TV show. She should encourage him to play with playmates. She should not use him as an escort for adult activities. It can never be a son's job to soothe his mother's emotional wounds, lift the burden of her loneliness, or listen to her while she vents about her frustrations.

The Natural Love Affair Between a Mother and Her Son

There is another side to the story. A mother should try to preserve the endearing love affair that any mother will naturally have with her son. She shouldn't suppress that out of fear of hurting him. It is in no way pathological for a mother and her son to take delight in each other, as long as the mother maintains the boundaries that keep it safe.

A little boy Charlie's age will often play at being his mother's special love and pretend husband, without wanting to, or being able to, actually take on the job. The good-enough mother knows this and lets her son have his play marriage, understanding that he needs it to seed his psyche for his adult relationships. The mother knows this is for the boy and not for her, except as a charmed onlooker. She knows he is not ready to be any adult woman's partner. Even if she is lonely and needy, she knows she must find other adults to satisfy that need in her.

Even though a boy naturally wants to be his mother's husband, the boy eventually accepts that he can't have her that way, if his father is present. He struggles to win against his father, but for his future emotional health and happiness, he must lose the struggle. He will learn that he can have her as his mother, but she is his father's wife. A good bond between father and mother naturally evokes the psychologically correct emotional boundaries. Otherwise, it takes more conscious thought on the part of the mother to make the home environment healthy for the boy.

How Contact with Men Will Help Your Son

A boy's contact with other men—grandfathers, uncles and other male relatives, coaches, and male teachers—can help him establish his masculine identity, especially if, in some of these relationships, the man shows a special interest in the boy while maintaining appropriate adult-child boundaries. Here, as with his mother, it is not healthy for a boy to try to take care of an adult's core needs, even if he "wants" to. Being with a child for an adult is an act of giving. The pleasure of being with a child is the pleasure of nurturing. It is the gardener's pleasure in helping something grow. Narcissistic people often have difficulty enjoying children, unless the children are admiring them.

However, contact with grandfathers, uncles, teachers, and other male mentors—no matter how appropriate and helpful to the development of the boy's positive masculine identity—cannot create the healthy adult intimacy boundary that makes mother-son enmeshment impossible. (See Figures 5-1 and 5-2.) If the mother is not in a stable relationship with a man, then she will need to take the special care that I've described in this chapter. With this extra awareness and care, she can and will avoid enmeshing her son.

The actress Kate Hudson (Goldie Hawn's daughter) eloquently expressed the importance to children of a strong mother-father bond in an interview in *The Reader's Digest:* ". . . our parents would go away and be lovers. We knew how important their relationship was, that their relationship was the foundation of our family. So, when we would see them go away for a weekend, we knew they were in love. We hated to see them leave, but it made us also know that they were two individuals who needed to be lovers, which felt great. It inspires you to have that in your life too."

SUMMARY:
HOW TO AVOID ENMESHING YOUR SON

1. *Be aware.* Your son will naturally want to "take care of his mommy," especially if he senses you are lonely and unhappy. Celebrate, but don't exploit, the love affair between you.

2. *Be reassuring.* You should explicitly tell your son, "It isn't your job to take care of me." Repeat when you see him struggling to find a way to make you feel better. Make sure you and he understand.

3. *Address his needs.* Let him play with his friends. If he tends to be alone, help him find friends to play with. When you spend "special time" with him, focus on what he needs or likes, not always what you need or like.

4. *Seek adult emotional support.* Look for emotionally supportive adult company inside and outside the house, including support groups and therapy. Never "vent" about your relationship or your troubles to your little boy, even if he seems eager to listen.

5. *Set healthy boundaries.* If you have an emotionally healthy man in your life, your little boy will more likely be protected from becoming a MEM. Otherwise, help him understand that he need not be, and cannot be, "mom's little man."

The Good-Enough Father

A boy needs a present and attentive father. This need begins at birth, although the newborn infant is more closely connected to his mother. By five, the need for the father intensifies. The boy naturally starts to want to merge more with the father, and he leaves the mother's realm, relatively speaking. Steve Biddulph gives the following progression in *Raising Boys: Why Boys Are Different—And How to Help Them Become Happy and Well-Balanced Men:* A boy is primarily attached to mother until he is five, to father from five until twelve, and, after that, to mentors. If the father is absent or distant when the boy is between the ages of five and twelve, then, by the time he is twelve, the boy is hungry for a father. He will be eager to become involved with male mentors, and he may not be very discriminating in his choices. He will be especially vulnerable to abuse by men who betray his trust.

Of course, a father can't just show up when the boy turns five and take over from the mother. He needs to be an ongoing presence. My son Zachary, who just turned four, is naturally identifying with me. This morning (at the time of writing) he wanted to dress like me. He wanted me to change my clothes, so that I would have on clothes like him. I was happy to do it. He hasn't turned five, but he needs me to be there for him.

How Can I Help My Wife Avoid Enmeshing Our Son?

If you fear that enmeshment is developing between your son and your wife (or ex-wife or partner or ex-partner), talk with her about what you are seeing. Explain your concerns about the way she is relating to your son. See if you can help her understand that your connection with your son is not a threat to her and is valuable to him. Most enmeshing mothers don't realize they are enmeshing and will be willing to reconsider how they are relating to their sons. If you don't seem to be able to help her understand what the problem is, see if she will come into counseling with you to discuss your "disagreement." This may be advisable, even if you are not living with your son's mother. I have counseled couples who sought joint therapy for the sake of their children even though they were divorced. Be prepared to weather her reactions when you first raise the issue of enmeshment. She might need to be defensive before she can listen to you.

The case where the enmeshing mother is completely uncooperative is difficult to manage. In this case, the father should seek professional advice, both psychological and legal. The other, and far more typical, situation is that stress and old trauma have led the mother to drift toward enmeshing her son and detaching from her husband, but she is not determined to do it. Here the father can intervene, both with the mother and with his son. This intervention will be critically important in stopping the enmeshment and preventing his son from growing up to be a MEM.

You might be worried that, by pressing her, you will be risking divorce, and if you divorce, you will be leaving your son with her all the time. That can happen, but you can't allow yourself to be intimidated into silence. This is too important for your son. You need to be prepared to challenge your wife. At the same time, let your son know that you want to spend time with him and you're not going to give up trying to make it happen. Usually the extreme reaction you fear doesn't happen. Typically, a mother is not aware she is enmeshing her son, and she will be willing to listen to you.

Make sure your relationship with your wife hasn't drifted into distance. Make a point of giving her lots of special time, so that she feels valued and to help her feel less lonely. Encourage her to get involved in some activities with her friends or at an organization where people socialize, like a church. Do something as a couple with other couples. When adults have adult relationships, they are less likely to turn to their children for companionship.

It could be that your wife will relapse into dependency with her son regularly. In spite of both your best intentions, it may just be something she has trouble with. In that case, you will need to run interference for your son on an ongoing basis. When he gets old enough, you can remind him: "I know your mother sometimes complains too much to you and is too intrusive. I'm working hard to make that stop, but I can't contain it all. I want you to know it's not fair to you. You have the right to know that." You can help him see the reality without putting his mother down. Say to him, "Even though you feel guilty, I want you to go out and enjoy your friends anyway. Your mother doesn't intend for you not to have friends. I'm going to continue to talk with her and help the situation the best I can."

Make sure you're giving him some *undivided* attention. Don't be preoccupied with your job or your hobby so that you ignore him when he is with you. He needs more than just an opportunity to be in your physical presence. He needs to know that you're connected to him and you've got his best interests in mind. Even though he gets overwhelmed by his mother, he knows that you are a lifeline for him. He needs to spend time with you when you are attuned to his needs and not yours.

If you are not living with your son, you still need to attempt to work cooperatively with his mother for his sake, as I've discussed. This may be challenging, if your relationship with her has included anger and frustration and negative encounters. You simply need to work with her to get beyond these bitter remnants of your past together so that your son's needs can be the priority. In extreme cases where his mother is uncooperative, it may be necessary to pursue court action to guarantee contact with your son.

SUMMARY:
How to Help Your Wife Avoid Enmeshing Your Son

1. *Recognize your importance.* You are important to your son. Be present and be attentive.

2. *Be reassuring.* Let your wife know you are not a threat to her relationship with your son. Be supportive of her so she doesn't feel alone.

3. *Recognize his needs.* When you spend "special time" with your son, focus on what he needs or likes, not always what you need or like.

4. *Seek your own emotional support.* Look for emotionally supportive adult company inside and outside the house, including support groups and therapy. Never "vent" about your wife or your troubles to your little boy, even if he seems eager to listen.

5. *Build a strong mother-father bond.* Nothing is more important to the emotional well-being of your son than a strong bond between his mother and his father.

Tell Your Children They Are Precious Cargo

As I was buckling my son, Zachary, in the car when he was three, he asked me, "Why do we wear seat belts, Daddy?"

I told him, "It's because you're my precious cargo."

Now, a year later, when I buckle him up, he says to me, "I'm your precious cargo, Daddy." So he's got it; he feels his special worth.

A lot of kids don't feel that. They have an emptiness at their core, and they keep this wound as adults. These wounded adults will defend against it either by becoming controlling and demanding, insisting that they be the center of attention without regard to other people's feelings, or by slipping to the other side and becoming retiring wallflowers, giving up their expectations that anyone will notice or attend to them.

The desire to be special is fundamental to all of us. We all need to feel that at our core we have value independent of what we do. My son now feels special for who he is. Whatever he does in later life, he will still think of himself as "special cargo."

It is never too late to help your son feel that he is special, by giving him the attention he craves and the respect for his boundaries he needs.

✑

The next chapter begins by noting how widespread mother-son enmeshment is in the world. It is a universal problem. We see Sonny and Anne one last time, as we summarize the main points of the book.

15 GETTING PAST ENMESHMENT
A New Freedom

Mother-son enmeshment is a problem that extends across cultures and across the world. A recent study by the Office of National Statistics in Britain shows that many British men live with their mothers well into adulthood: three out of four to age twenty-five and one in eight until age thirty.

According to Rebecca Pike and Carmel Allen in their article, "Mamma Mia," Italian men daily seek their mothers' advice on what to wear, what to eat, and who to socialize with. "Throughout their married life it isn't [his wife] he turns to for advice, but his mother." Further, many Italian couples have problems caused by interference from the husband's mother. "In Italy it is said to be the cause of relationship breakdowns in 36 percent of cases, compared with 25 percent in Germany and 18 percent in France."

Mother-son enmeshment is also embedded in Japanese culture, according to psychologists Adams and Hill. They report that Japanese women "live vicariously through their offspring, perhaps especially their sons. . . . Japanese mothers commonly view their children as an extension of themselves. . . . Since marriage offers so little in the way of satisfaction, they may also bind their children to them in a desperate effort to find some measure of pleasure, solace, and comfort. . . . Lacking [satisfaction] in marriage, Japanese mothers discover substitute satisfactions with their offspring. . . . Independent existence [for the child] is unacceptable."

These reports, along with others, suggest that mother-son enmeshment is common in the world. Is there some broader meaning to this trend? I believe it is a symptom of a worldwide growth in societal detachment.

It is primarily through friends and family that humans have sustained themselves emotionally in the past. But today substitutes for human connections—alcohol, drugs, television, careers, the Internet—are freely available. Although these things are less satisfying than human contact, their use dulls awareness that the need for human contact is not being met. Lonely men can make do with lives focused on work and pornography and imagine that nothing is amiss. Lonely mothers can turn to their little boys for emotional support, not realizing the potential damage that can result.

A Last Session with Sonny and Anne

Global mother-son enmeshment was on my mind when I met for the last time with Sonny and Anne. We had actually finished nearly a year before, but they wanted a last session, just a few weeks before their marriage ceremony, to celebrate and reflect on their long therapeutic journey.

"I was so scared," Anne said. "I knew I loved this man. I knew I deserved to have a relationship with him, and I knew he wanted to have one with me. But he couldn't see it. And I took a chance on both of us by coming to see you. You helped me see I could let the relationship go, if I had to, but I could fight for it first. And I did, and here we are. And I'm just so grateful to you, Dr. Adams, and I'm certainly grateful to you, Sonny." She had to stop, because she had begun to cry.

Sonny had begun to tear up too, and he took Anne's hand. "You know," he said, "I had no idea what was going on." He stopped to consider this while Anne wiped her eyes. "I guess I did," he decided, "but I really didn't want to see it.

"I've never felt so free in my life to love somebody, and I love you," he said to her. "I hated the way you were so pushy." He grinned, and she smiled. "I was angry about that, but deep down I knew you were right. You were persistent—in a nice way—and I finally got it.

"You helped me to stay with it," he said to me. "I wasn't happy with Mom dominating my life, but I didn't want to disappoint her. I didn't want to think about it. Then I got it, with your help. I could love my mother and not have to jump every time she called. I thought that was impossible. Mom's not exactly happy about it, but that's okay. When she complains, I say, 'We've crossed that bridge. You know I love you.' She grumbles, but I'm not afraid of that reaction the way I used to be."

I was impressed with how different this Sonny was from the one I had first met three years before. Then he thought he didn't have a problem and he didn't need to talk about it. Now he's in full charge of his relationship with his mother.

I had enjoyed working with Sonny and Anne. They were a likable couple, and it had been great seeing them come together, when they had been on the verge of splitting up.

"It's really amazing to have watched how both of you have changed," I told them. "In the beginning you were so tenuous about your relationship. You were ready to leave each other. It took a lot of courage to confront this." I turned to Anne. "You were gentle with Sonny, but very clear. That clarity was the foundation of everything that followed. And now you're getting married."

"And we can't wait to have a family," said Sonny. "We're going to have kids. I'm going to be a dad." Anne was blushing at this, but she smiled with him. "Those are going to be lucky kids," he went on, "because we know what they need. We respect each other, and we know about boundaries. We aren't going to pass this trouble down to our children. It stops with us." Sonny was grinning at me and Anne, like a kid who had just made A on his algebra final.

But his words made me think.

A Mother of Valor Turns the Room Silent

After my first book, *Silently Seduced,* was published, I was giving many public lectures and conference talks. At one conference for professional therapists, I was speaking to a group of about a hundred people. There were a number of questions after the talk, and then a woman held up her hand. I called on her, expecting another question. But she made a statement instead.

"My name is . . ." and she identified herself. "I'm a therapist," she went on, "and I've been doing this to my son." The whole room suddenly became silent. She went on, "I'm calling for an appointment with a therapist as soon as I leave here, and it's going to stop today. I know what my little boy needs, and I'm going to give it to him. I'm so grateful you opened my eyes about this."

It was a courageous, wonderful moment for this woman and for her son and for everyone listening. She was responding to her new awareness with a pledge to take action and make things better. She understood that she wasn't being blamed; rather she was being offered the opportunity to help her child. She was putting the needs of her son ahead of her own.

Aware mothers are the key to ending mother-son enmeshment, but fathers are also critically important. Their abandonment of their families creates the vacuum that makes enmeshment possible. I'd like all fathers to stop to think, before they bolt for a new woman or quit therapy: You have a huge responsibility here. You too can find some freedom and some love with your wife that you might never discover if you run away. Even more significant, you can be the deciding vote on whether your children have a future of hope or a future of disappointment.

A Call to Consciousness

It is critical for us to stay mindful of our attachments, of the importance of building adult relationships and having them be primary, and not turning to children inappropriately. Attachments are really the life raft through life's troubles. If you look at the models for successful recovery from addictions, they all include the building of community. Twelve-step groups are primarily communities. Without community, most addicts relapse. And there's a reason for that. Healthy attachments are fundamental to emotional happiness.

Coming to consciousness is the key to emotional freedom. With consciousness comes awareness; with awareness, the possibility of action; with action, the opportunity for change; and with change, the option to make things better. You have seen many troubles, but you can make things better. Have the courage to be aware, and your heart will be opened to true love and commitment.

NOTES

Full information for references is given in the bibliography.

Chapter 1

For the section "When A MEM Wants a Wife": *Psycho,* director Alfred Hitchcock, screenplay Joseph Stefano (from novel by Robert Block), Paramount/MCA Universal, 1960.

For the section "A Place in His Heart": *The Sopranos,* executive producers: David Chase, Brad Grey, Ilene S. Landress, Terence Winter. New York: Home Box Office Original Programming/Brad Grey Television and Chase Films, 2000–2007.

Chapter 2

For the box "Addictions": For an in-depth consideration of psychological trauma and addictions, see Tian Dayton's *Trauma and Addiction: Ending the Cycle of Pain Through Emotional Literacy.*

Chapter 3

For the section "Adolescence and Individuation": Erik H. Erikson formulated the stages of childhood development and the difficulties that arise for an individual who does not transition through the stages satisfactorily. This understanding of the stages of childhood development, and the troubles that come to individuals when stages are disrupted or not completed satisfactorily, is a key insight for psychotherapy. Erikson's ideas are given a clear and readable explanation by John and Linda Friel in their book on dysfunctional families, *Adult Children: The Secrets of Dysfunctional Families.*

Chapter 7

For the section "How to Court a Woman": Courting difficulties have been discussed in the context of cybersex addiction. See Patrick Carnes et al., *In the Shadows of the Net.*

Chapter 8

For the section "What's Wrong with Roles?": John and Linda Friel in their book *Adult Children* talk about "dysfunctional roles" on p. 57.

Chapter 9

For the box "Projecting Feelings": In clinical circles, the word "projection" means attributing your feelings to someone else: "I hate you, so you must hate me." This is not the sense in which I am using the concept of "projection" or "projecting feelings."

Chapter 14

For the section "The Enmeshing Mother and the Good-Enough Mother": From *A Secure Base* by John Bowlby, p. 150: "A parent may have sought to make one of her children her attachment figure by discouraging him from exploring the world away from her and from believing that he will ever be able to make his way on his own."

For the section "How Can I Avoid Enmeshing My Son": Kate Hudson interview, *Reader's Digest* (June 2004), p. 98. Ms. Hudson's comments are about her single mother, Goldie Hawn, and her mother's longtime partner, the actor Kurt Russell, whom Hudson identifies in the article as "Dad."

Chapter 15

For the first paragraph: Sanjay Suri, India Abroad News Service, August 9, 2000.

For the second paragraph: Rebecca Pike and Carmel Allen, "Mamma Mia," *The Guardian,* May 14, 2002.

For the third paragraph: Kenneth Alan Adams, Ph.D., and Lester Hill, Jr., Ph.D., "Castration Anxiety in Japanese Group Fantasies," *Digital Archive of Psychohistory* 26, no. 4 (Spring 1999).

RECOMMENDED READING

The following books have been particularly helpful to my clients and their partners. See the bibliography for publication information.

Parent-Child Enmeshment

My previous book on enmeshment, *Silently Seduced: When Parents Make Their Children Partners—Understanding Covert Incest,* looks at enmeshment from the perspective of parent-child incest. I use the term "covert incest" to distinguish enmeshment from physical incest. When a parent uses a child as a surrogate husband or wife, the child will develop in adulthood a definite collection of problems that are similar to the problems of adults who suffered physical incest. I spend considerable time on the aspect of wounded sexuality. For some MEM, this perspective is very clarifying. *Silently Seduced* has a recovery-oriented perspective and would be especially useful to MEM who are in recovery programs.

The Emotional Incest Syndrome: What to Do When a Parent's Love Rules Your Life, by Pat Love and Jo Robinson, describes parent-child enmeshment from the perspective of family systems, looking at roles children are forced to play when emotional incest is a part of the family dynamics. This book offers a number of helpful insights on how to resolve unhealthy family patterns that have resulted from parent-child enmeshment.

Relationships

The 7 Best Things Happy Couples Do, by John and Linda Friel, describes in a friendly, informal style the core issues that all couples face:

for example, people always pair up with their emotional equals, a concept that is critical in understanding relationship patterns. The Friels present some strong and surprising general principles, such as the fact that the willingness to get divorced is a keystone of a happy marriage. This book is readable, hopeful, and practical. A MEM and his partner can find no better guide to help them navigate through the relationship issues they will inevitably face.

Getting the Love You Want: A Guide for Couples, by Harville Hendrix, describes the "Imago therapy" approach to keeping relationships healthy. It identifies each partner as being both a source of emotional pain and a source of healing for each other. Hendrix develops this apparent contradiction in justifying and explaining his approach. He describes specific techniques, such as the couples dialogue, to help a couple turn conflicts into opportunities for strengthening the relationship. This is a practical guide for couples to understand and benefit from their conflicts.

Melody Beattie's *Codependent No More: How to Stop Controlling Others and Start Caring for Yourself* is the classic self-help book on codependency. It gives a step-by-step process for identifying when someone is lost in an obsessive focus on another person and how to break free. Chronic codependency is one of the dysfunctional relationship patterns most common in MEM. MEM are often codependent with their mothers, their partners, their siblings, their coworkers, and others. Partners of MEM are also prone to codependency.

The Betrayal Bond: Breaking Free of Exploitive Relationships, by Patrick Carnes, explains why people can be loyal to situations or people that are harmful to them. Carnes provides specific assessment tools and suggestions on how to deal with betrayal bonds. A MEM has been forced by his enmeshment to declare loyalty to his mother, a relationship in which he has been both betrayed and harmed. Not only is this a "betrayal bond" itself, but also the MEM tends later in life to be drawn to other such relationships, with women, at work, and in social situations. Therefore, understanding his tendency to make betrayal bonds will be especially useful to a MEM. The partners of a MEM may find this book useful also if she has a history of betrayal bonding.

Is It Love or Is It Addiction? by Brenda Schaeffer clarifies and distinguishes healthy love from the obsessive dependency that is often called love in our culture. This self-help book gives specific characteristics of addictive love and healthy love, and it provides tools for self-assessment. MEM are prone to developing unhealthy dependencies. This book will help them, and their partners, understand the difference between addictive love and healthy love.

The Seven Principles for Making Marriage Work, by John Gottman and Nan Silver, outlines the habits of successful married couples. The authors give seven specific principles for marital harmony and lasting love. The book features practical questionnaires and exercises that a couple can use to advance their mutual understanding.

Narcissists

Nina Brown's *Children of the Self-Absorbed: A Grownup's Guide to Getting Over Narcissistic Parents* carefully presents the characteristics of narcissistic parents and the symptoms that children of narcissists will typically carry into adulthood. The book includes information on how to recover from a childhood dominated by narcissists and also on managing relationships with narcissistic parents in adulthood. Many MEM have narcissistic parents, and this book will help them better understand what happened and what to do about it.

The Wizard of Oz and Other Narcissists: Coping with the One-Way Relationship in Work, Love, and Family, by Eleanor Payson, uses the metaphor of the Wizard of Oz for the all-powerful, domineering, "knows he's right and he doesn't want to listen to you" narcissistic person. This book explains in clear detail what narcissistic people are like and what happens to others who are involved with them. There is a chapter on narcissistic parenting, which is particularly relevant for MEM. Payson describes what it is like to be with a narcissist: "Soon the lion's share of attention and resources are going in one direction— toward the narcissist. When involved with a narcissist, the damage to your own self-esteem can be enormous, resulting in chronic anger, depression, and feelings of helplessness." When the mother of a small child is a narcissist, the enmeshment wounds will be that much more severe.

Addictions and Recovery

Out of the Shadows: Understanding Sexual Addiction is the first in a series of books authored by Patrick Carnes on the subject of sexual addiction. This book helped define, justify, and popularize the term "sexual addiction" for compulsive sexual behaviors. Carnes does an excellent job of describing the addictive process and how to recover from it. This book is a must-read for anyone who is dealing with compulsive sexual thoughts and behaviors.

Sexual Anorexia: Overcoming Sexual Self-Hatred, by Patrick Carnes with Joseph Moriarity, describes the important but rarely discussed problems of people who have shut down sexually and avoid expressing their sexuality. The book gives specific exercises to help people become more comfortable with themselves and reclaim their sexual desire. MEM and partners who have lost the sexual element of their relationship will find this book helpful.

In the Shadows of the Net: Breaking Free of Compulsive Online Sexual Behavior is about excessive use of cybersex. Carnes and his co-authors describe how to discriminate among those who use cybersex recreationally, those who are vulnerable to becoming addicted, and those who are sexually addicted and are using the Internet to accelerate their addiction. This book also offers compassionate insights and guidance to working through the process of recovery. I recommend this book to people who think they or a loved one may have a compulsive problem with cybersex. It is also useful for partners, since it describes how people feel who are involved with cybersex addicts.

Men

I Don't Want to Talk About It, by Terrence Real, describes both overt ("recognized") and covert ("unrecognized") depression. This latter he calls "masked depression," because workaholism, raging, or abusive behaviors often mask it. These acting-out responses to covert depression have been identified as "masculine issues," whereas depression was in the past incorrectly identified as a "woman's issue." The book offers specific suggestions for making things better, and it would be useful for any MEM who suspects he may be depressed.

Iron John, by Robert Bly, describes in a poetic metaphor important truths about coming of age for boys. It is the story of a boy who has to leave the realm of his mother to be initiated into the world of men. MEM frequently do not have a strong and comfortable identification with their fathers and/or other male mentors. This book will help them discover and honor their need for a strong masculine identity.

Dysfunctional Families

John and Linda Friel's *Adult Children: The Secrets of Dysfunctional Families* describes the effects in adulthood of having grown up in a dysfunctional family system. This book focuses on the *roles* that children take on in such families, including the surrogate-husband roles of mother-son enmeshment. *Adult Children* is written in a straightforward, readable, informal style that takes readers through what would otherwise be complicated clinical concepts. It's filled with suggestions to get past dysfunctional habits and feelings. It would be appropriate for MEM and their partners who want to understand dysfunctional families from a broader perspective than enmeshment.

Sexual Abuse

Beyond Betrayal, by Richard Gartner, describes childhood sexual abuse of boys, including the impact of boyhood sexual abuse and steps for healing. The book is compassionate, insightful, and hopeful in dealing with this difficult topic. It is a necessary book for any MEM whose enmeshment crossed the line into sexual abuse, such as Freddy (Chapter 7).

Shame

Healing the Shame That Binds You, by John Bradshaw, is a classic recovery guide. In it Bradshaw defines "toxic shame," in contrast to healthy shame, and he identifies toxic shame as a powerful destructive force. He explains how it is generated in dysfunctional family systems and describes approaches to healing. This book will be particularly helpful to MEM, or their partners, who have found themselves bound up in issues related to shame.

BIBLIOGRAPHY

Adams, Kenneth M. *Silently Seduced: When Parents Make Their Children Partners—Understanding Covert Incest*. Deerfield Beach, FL: Health Communications, 1991.

Beattie, Melody. *Codependent No More: How to Stop Controlling Others and Start Caring for Yourself*. New York: Harper & Row, 1987.

Biddulph, Steve. *Raising Boys: Why Boys Are Different—and How to Help Them Become Happy and Well-Balanced Men*. Berkeley, CA: Celestial Arts, 1998.

Bly, Robert. *Iron John: A Book about Men*. New York: Addison-Wesley, 1990.

Bowlby, John. *Separation Anxiety and Anger*. New York: Basic Books, 1973.

Bowlby, John. *A Secure Base: Parent-Child Attachment and Healthy Human Development*. New York: Basic Books, 1988.

Bradshaw, John. *Healing the Shame that Binds You*. Deerfield Beach, FL: Health Communications, 1988.

Brown, Nina W. *Children of the Self-Absorbed: A Grownup's Guide to Getting Over Narcissistic Parents*. Oakland, CA: Harbinger, 2001.

Carnes, Patrick. *The Betrayal Bond: Breaking Free of Exploitive Relationships*. Deerfield Beach, FL: Health Communications, 1997.

Carnes, Patrick, *Out of the Shadows: Understanding Sexual Addiction*. Minneapolis: CompCare Publishers, 1983.

Carnes, Patrick, with Joseph M. Moriarity. *Sexual Anorexia: Overcoming Sexual Self-Hatred*. Center City, MN: Hazelden, 1997.

Carnes, Patrick, David L. Delmonico, and Elizabeth Griffin, with Joseph M. Moriarity. *In the Shadows of the Net: Breaking Free of Compulsive Online Sexual Behavior.* Center City, MN: Hazelden, 2001.

Cozzens, Donald B. *The Changing Face of the Priesthood.* Collegeville, PA: The Liturgical Press, 2000.

Dayton, Tian. *Trauma and Addiction: Ending the Cycle of Pain through Emotional Literacy.* Deerfield Beach, FL: Health Communications, 2000.

Forward, Susan. *Toxic Parents.* New York: Bantam Books, 2002.

Fossum, Merle A., and Marilyn J. Mason. *Facing Shame: Families in Recovery.* New York: W. W. Norton, 1986.

Friel, John and Linda. *Adult Children: The Secrets of Dysfunctional Families.* Pompano Beach, FL: Health Communications, 1988.

Friel, John and Linda. *The 7 Best Things Happy Couples Do.* Deerfield Beach, FL: Health Communications, 2002.

Gartner, Richard B. *Betrayed as Boys: Psychodynamic Treatment of Sexually Abused Men.* New York: Guilford Press, 1999.

Gartner, Richard B. *Beyond Betrayal: Taking Charge of Your Life after Boyhood Sexual Abuse.* Hoboken, NJ: John Wiley & Sons, 2005.

Gorodensky, Arlene. *Mum's the Word: The Mamma's Boy Syndrome Revealed.* London: Cassell, 1997.

Gottman, John M., and Nan Silver. *The Seven Principles for Making Marriage Work.* New York: Three Rivers Press, 1999.

Grizzle, Anne F., and William Proctor. *Mothers Who Love Too Much: Breaking Dependent Love Patterns in Family Relationships.* New York: Ivy Books, 1988.

Gurian, Michael. *Mothers, Sons & Lovers: How a Man's Relationship with His Mother Affects the Rest of His Life.* Boston: Shambhala Publications, 1994.

Haffner, Debra W. *From Diapers to Dating: A Parent's Guide to Raising Sexually Healthy Children.* New York: Newmarket Press, 2000.

Hendrix, Harville. *Getting the Love You Want: A Guide for Couples.* New York: Owl Books; 2001 (reprint).

Kindlon, Dan, and Michael Thompson. *Raising Cain: Protecting the Emotional Life of Boys.* New York: Ballantine, 2000.

Lee, John. *The Flying Boy.* Deerfield Beach, FL: Health Communications, 1989.

Love, Patricia, and Jo Robinson. *The Emotional Incest Syndrome: What to Do When a Parent's Love Rules Your Life.* New York: Bantam Books, 1991.

Mellody, Pia, with Andrea Wells Miller and J. Keith Miller. *Facing Love Addiction: Giving Yourself the Power to Change the Way You Love.* New York: HarperCollins, 1992.

Miller, Alice. *The Drama of the Gifted Child: The Search for the True Self.* New York: Basic Books, 1981.

Money, John. *Lovemaps: Clinical Concepts of Sexual/Erotic Health and Pathology, Paraphilia and Gender Transportation in Childhood, Adolescence and Maturity.* New York: Irvington Publishers, 1993.

Monick, Eugene. *Castration and Male Rage: The Phallic Wound.* Toronto: Inner City Books, 1991.

Nouwen, Henry J. M. *Intimacy.* San Francisco: Harper, 1981.

Payson, Eleanor D. *The Wizard of Oz and Other Narcissists: Coping with One-Way Relationship in Work, Love, and Family.* Royal Oak, MI: Julian Day Publications, 2002.

Real, Terrence. *I Don't Want to Talk About It: Overcoming the Secret Legacy of Male Depression.* New York: Fireside, 1997.

Schaeffer, Brenda. *Is It Love or Is It Addiction?* Center City, MN: Hazelden, 1997.

Schore, A. N. *Affect Dysregulation and Disorders of the Self* and *Affect Regulation and the Repair of the Self* (2-volume Set). New York: W. W. Norton, 2003.

Schwartz, M. F., and S. Southern. "Manifestations of Damaged Development of the Human Affectional Systems and Developmentally Based Psychotherapies," *Sexual Addiction & Compulsivity: The Journal of Treatment and Prevention* 3 (1999), 163–175.

Sipe, Richard A. W. *A Secret World: Sexuality and the Search for Celibacy.* New York: Brunner/Mazel, 1990.

Trachtenberg, Peter. *The Casanova Complex: Compulsive Lovers and Their Women.* New York: Poseidon Press, 1988.

Viorst, Judith. *Necessary Losses: The Loves, Illusions, Dependencies and Impossible Expectations That All of Us Have to Give Up in Order to Grow.* New York: Simon & Schuster, 1986.

Wallerstein, Judith S., and Sandra Blakeslee. *The Good Marriage: How and Why Love Lasts.* New York: Warner Books, 1996.

Whitfield, Charles L. *Boundaries and Relationships: Knowing, Protecting and Enjoying the Self.* Deerfield Beach, FL: Health Communications, 1993.

RESOURCES

Website for *When He's Married to Mom:*
www.whenhesmarriedtomom.com

Post your questions for Dr. Adams to answer. Read other people's questions
and Dr. Adams's answers. This site also features the latest information on
parent-child enmeshment and a calendar of workshops, classes, and lectures.

Sex Addicts Anonymous (SAA)
PO Box 70949
Houston, TX 77270
(800) 477-8191 or (713) 869-4902
www.saa-recovery.org

Codependents of Sexual Addiction (COSA)
PO Box 14537
Minneapolis, MN 55414
(763) 537-6904
www.cosa-recovery.org

Society for the Advancement of Sexual Health (SASH)
PO Box 725544
Atlanta, GA 31139
(770) 541-9912
www.sash.net

Sexaholics Anonymous (SA)
International Central Office
PO Box 3565
Brentwood, TN 37024
(615) 370-6062 or (866) 424-8777
www.sa.org

S-Anon (Partners)
PO Box 111242
Nashville, TN 37222-1242
(800) 210-8141 or (615) 833-3152
www.sanon.org

Sex and Love Addicts Anonymous (SLAA)
Fellowship-Wide Services
1550 NE Loop 410, Suite 118
San Antonio, TX 78209
(210) 828-7900
www.slaafws.org

Codependents Anonymous (CODA)
Fellowship Services Office
PO Box 33577
Phoenix, AZ 85067-3577
(602) 277-7991
www.coda.org

Recovering Couples Anonymous (RCA)
PO Box 11029
Oakland, CA 94611
(510) 663-2312
www.recovering-couples.org

National Association for Children of Alcoholics (NACOA)
11426 Rockville Pike, Suite 301
Rockville, MD 20852
(888) 55-4COAS or (301) 468-0985
www.nacoa.org

Overeaters Anonymous
World Service Office
PO Box 44020
Rio Rancho, NM 87174-4020
(505) 891-2664
www.oa.org

Alcoholics Anonymous (AA)
AA World Services, Inc.
PO Box 459
New York, NY 10163
(212) 870-3400
www.alcoholics-anonymous.org

Al-Anon/Alateen
Al-Anon Family Group Headquarters, Inc.
1600 Corporate Landing Parkway
Virginia Beach, VA 23454-5617
(757) 563-1600
www.al-anon.org

National Organization Against Male Sexual Victimization
Male Survivor
PMB 103
5505 Connecticut Avenue, NW
Washington, DC 20015-2601
(800) 738-4181
www.malesurvivor.org

Website by Dr. Patrick Carnes with information on sexual addiction:
www.sexhelp.com

INDEX